Lulu Press
www.lulu.com

For orders, contact the publisher at the address above.
ISBN 978-1-304-24511-3

Printed in the United States of America

Women Talk Too Damn Much! Reclaiming Self, Love, Intimacy, and the Ultimate Connection

By

Zoe Spencer

2

Acknowledgements

I would first like to thank my future daughter in law, Chaquena Bell, for telling me "Ma you should write an answer to Steve Harvey's book" and always encouraging and motivating me to grow. I would like to thank my son Olando ReChaud for continuing to serve as an example of what "a good man" is in all senses of the word man. I would like to thank my eternal readers, my God Daughters Adrienne and Alexis for always being interested and taking the time to read what I wrote. And most importantly, I would again like to thank my students at Virginia State University-specifically all of my students in Social Psychology- for giving me the fuel that I needed to construct this work...and my students at Cheyney University for also serving as a foundation...

Thank you Gerald Evans, of Gerald Evans photography, for the beautiful cover photo...

Not forsaking the most important part of my being God for His continued guidance and presence in my inner and outer space. I love you all immensely.

Preface
Mr. Right Now

Although I am not a man, I venture into this work with full confidence, that like a man, I too understand what men think. But, even more significantly, I venture into this work with full understanding that as a woman, I know what it means to be a single woman struggling to find "the one," a married woman trying to "make it work," a single mom trying to stay afloat, and a heart broken woman trying to find its meaning. I understand the complicated balancing act that it requires to navigate and negotiate one's way through the *dating scene*- in all of its forms, from the internet to the club, and then the *dating game*- in all of its forms, from the "booty call" to "almost married," and finally through *the heartbreak* that always seems to be inevitable in one shape or form at some point in almost every woman's life- from the let down to the divorce. In essence, I have done it all.

More importantly than my own personal experiences though, I have been blessed with the opportunity to not only have done my own self evaluation and intra-reflection in my attempts to find my "self," and prepare *me* for the beautiful happily ever after that I have been socialized to believe in; but, I have helped countless numbers of other people- family, friends, clients, colleagues, and students work through it all. I have literally had thousands of discussions with heartbroken or searching women and men. I have taught many courses such as *Marriage and the Family, Social Psychology, Psychology, and Sociology*- where I have guided discussions on relationship dynamics. I have had many informal focus groups with college students about their concepts of love, commitment, sex and intimacy, and given and participated in (and continue to give and participate in) countless numbers of speeches, panel discussions on love, loving self, relationship dynamics, and women's and men's issues. But, more importantly I have cried on the phone and on the couches with my own sisters and "girlz" since I was a pre teen. So, I am confident that I am qualified to participate in and contribute to the discussion on love and relationships.

However, it is has taken me this long to finally sit down to write this book because in spite of it all, I just did not have the motivation. It was just so much easier to talk about it, lecture about it, "therapize" the few, until two things happened- a class discussion at Virginia State University and reading Steve Harvey's book. And it's funny because the two collided at the same moment and gave me the burst of energy that I needed to finally compose this feisty love song.

It was on a Sunday night. Although I was sleeping, like I do when I have not completed what I am supposed to do, I was preparing for class the next day. The topic for the next two weeks was developing interpersonal relationships. The topic for the class was "What is Love?" I was trying to decide whether I wanted to simply use the approach that I had used so many times before-that is asking the class to define love- or do something different. I knew that like every time before, and I do mean *every* time before, if I allowed my students (who are on an average between the ages of 18-21 years old as the general age range) to lead the discussion on what is love, it would only turn into a sidetracked heated debate between the young men and young women who really do not have the experience or insight to develop holistic and healthy definitions of love, much less discuss them. Hell, even people my age have difficulty. So, I guess subconsciously, I was attempting to develop my own definition- something that could guide the discussion, or at the least provide a grounded definition of love that the conversation could feed off of. And I did-at 3:30 in the morning. Not only did I come up with a definition of love, but I also went a step further to construct a definition of "making love."

That morning I wrote the definition of love on the board, and broke it down for the class. The following class, I separated the men and the women and asked them to, as a segregated group, based on the definition of love that I had constructed, construct a definition of "making love" and to list the characteristics that two people would have to share and/or a partner would have to have in order to share the experience of making love. In essence, yet without saying, I was asking the class to define what qualities and characteristics were essential to loving and making love to someone.

I pause here..

Because most men, who would even venture to open the cover of this book, feeling that it is just another male bashing book, would close the book at the end of the last sentence. And most women's mouths are watering for the "man bashing session" that they think is to come between the covers of this book. Why? Because most people would believe that it would be the young men who would have had difficulty with the assignment-that their "masculine" definition would be some superficial definition that is mired in their strictly physical, sexual, or "doggish" approach toward love, intimacy, and more importantly women. But, I had hypothesized differently, even before I constructed the assignment. And I was correct.

I sat in the middle of the room and passively observed each group, paying more close attention to the young men's process. They easily came up with a very direct definition of making love (which will be discussed in the next chapter), and were very clear about the qualities that a woman had to have in order for them to "make love"- a definition that was clearly based on their idea of love. The women, on the other hand, in an answer to "what qualities must a man have in order for you to 'make love' to him?" came up with the definition for what they termed "*Mr. Right Now.*"

Their collective definition of the qualities that it would take were: A man would have to be attractive, know tricks (sexually), have game, be the type that would get bored with a relationship, and be the 20 % in the 80/20 rule. I am not kidding, that was the definition that they collectively came up with. Now of course, when I got ready to critique it, some wanted to jump off of the sinking boat, but I was observing and everybody was rowing- none actively expressed opposition to the definition or jumped off of the boat before it started to sink.

Now although I know that this is an extreme, and that most women will completely deny that that's the way that *they* feel, it was important for one very specific reason. It was a verbal reflection of how women act. Yes. Don't get mad. *That* definition was a verbal reflection of the fact that in today's era, where more and more women are getting disheartened and farther removed from the reality that true love, good and faithful men, and beautiful, committed relationships are possible, *we* (women) are trying to put up the facade that we are able to play "the game" based on our perception of what we think men want. In essence, in our own self inflicted confusion, we are trying to act like men- which leads to the collision with Harvey's book.

The conflict is that we are not men. Not only that, as Harvey points out in his book, *Act Like A Lady*, (key word) '*Think' Like A Man*, we don't even have a healthy perception or understanding of what men *really* think. However, even worse is the fact that many women don't even have a healthy perception about how a "lady" is supposed to act. But, I still stuttered to write this book because I was convinced that Harvey had it. Upon reading Harvey's book, I was hoping to get a more grounded understanding of what men think. I was hoping that he would provide that epiphany by "gut punching" us (women) the way we needed to be punched in order to stop blaming men and start looking at or within ourselves for the answers.

But, Harvey's book didn't do it *for me*, in spite of the hype. I did not think that Harvey's work was sufficient in changing women's perception of what men think because it really didn't tell us anything new about our perceptions of men. As a matter of fact, to me, it only reinforced the same generalized perceptions (stereotypes) of men at their different levels-from mama's boy, the "commitment-phobics," to not deep (or dogs) by nature. So, to me, it only served to, in essence teach/train women how to negotiate those stereotypical perceptions of men in a more self-centered way as opposed to giving *us* the reality check that *we need* about self in order to negotiate the whole nature of relationships. It addressed the reality that we (women) are our own worse enemies, but it did not get to the root of why, because it kind of blamed men for the issues that women create and/or enable. And, to me, it did not quite give men the credit that they have truly earned.

The reality of it is that most men have very grounded perceptions of love and commitment. Many are not afraid of either word. Many are open to the possibility of

8

love. And most have a very consistent and strict set of criteria for the woman that they will be open to truly loving and committing to. So contrary to what many women believe, there is not a canine gene attached to the Y chromosome. It is not in a man's inherent or innate nature to be "a dog," a strictly sexual or physical being, or to be naturally fearful or avoidant of a commitment/relationship/or marriage. Men are not from Mars, they are from Earth, just like we are. That is why when they find "that one," they do not hesitate to take that stand at the altar next to the Pastor, Rabbi, Priest, sit in front of the Imam, or even stand before the Magistrate-even when it is not with *you/us/me or her*.

However, women make it difficult for a man to "go there" because (1) we think we are flawless and do it all right, (2) we *think* we know what men want and think, so (3) we don't listen, and when we want someone, we (4) become impatient, competitive, and even irrational so (5) instead of being true to our selves, we become what, not who, we mistakenly think men want us to be, and in such, (6) we refuse to value our own selves above our perception of how others value us. Consequently, (7) we set such a collective pattern of physicality and superficiality in our interaction with men, that we can not lay the foundation for the beautiful relationships that we "say" or even deny we want.

In essence, we are counterproductive to our own goal because we are too busy *"feeling" like a woman*, while we are *"acting" like a man."*

Chapter 1
In Defense of My Brothers, This is What They Said

<u>Women Talk Too Damn Much!</u>

When it comes to relationship dynamics, intimacy, and understanding love, one of the most important skills that a woman can develop and cultivate is her ability to *actively* listen to what men are saying. I am <u>not</u> talking about listening with the perception and answer intact, or the rebuttal already revving so loudly in our own minds that we cannot possibly hear or process what he is saying-because we already know what men think, we *read the book*. I am <u>not</u> talking about listening ---for the pause, waiting for him to take the slightest little breath --- so we can jump in and invoke our own perceptions and opinions. I am talking about sitting back and listening, not just hearing with our ears, but listening with all of our senses and processing with an open (not a closed) mind.

We can't even "play" the dating game because we don't have an accurate perception of who men really are, what men really want, what they think, what motivates them, what drives them, what makes him marry her instead of you. We really DO NOT know the rules. So even when we *think* we are "playing" the game, or even "playing" men, we end up playing our "selves" because we didn't have the object, rules, or boundaries of the game right. That's why we ran to Harvey's book. Well, Harvey told us what men think, let me tell you what they said.

Just like it is said of women, men will tell you everything you need to know! They can and will express *exactly* how they feel if we just sit back and lis-ten. And unlike our process, we don't even have to listen that long, or de-code the cipher, because they

10

are very clear and concise in their manner of communication. Their communication and conflict resolution style is "get in and get out"-simply. They say exactly what they mean and feel in as few words as possible, that is- when they do not feel threatened or defensive by their perception of what our response will be. That is why we must not create a hostile communication environment *if* we want to hear/know the truth. It is not that men are simple; because like us, they are multidimensional and heterogeneous beings. They just *say* and *express* what they mean **simply.**

The reason why men learn so much about us, and we can't seem to figure them out" without reading a book about it-the reason why they are able to play us so well, (when they choose to) is simply because we (women) talk too damn much! We have not cultivated or developed, much less mastered the art of listening AT ALL. We don't listen with and/or to our fathers, husbands, boyfriends, sons, male friends, co-workers, class mates, acquaintances, or the drunken men at the bar. We just like to talk, to express how we *feel*. So, men have learned to just let us talk. They gather the information, process it, store it, and use it to internally gauge how they will "manage" (and/or manipulate) us.

One of the most common and prevalent perceptions and themes that men have about women is that you can't win an argument with a woman, so don't even try. Even the elders train and queue the young men in this tradition. And when men say it, women respond to the testimony with fervor as if it is the gospel. Can the congregation say AMEN! A-MEN! Men say. "Even when a woman is wrong, just don't argue. Let her say what she wants, and just do what you gonna do." And the fact that most women rally around this perceived accomplishment is telling.

Even when we *are* wrong, we'd rather "win" the argument than to let a man tell us how wrong we are, much less acknowledge that we are wrong, not just to them, but even to our own selves. So we will keep it going-even if that means changing the subject and bringing up something he did to take the focus off of us, when it is feeling too much like a loss. The same thing we accuse men of. So, I have to agree with their analysis because I have not only been the "talk too much perpetrator," but it is an undeniable, significant, and prevalent pattern in interaction and communication dynamics between men and women-from the classroom to the bedroom. And we think this won't have an impact?

I have seen it in just about every forum and scenario from my own family, friends, clients, and students. The dynamics are so pervasive. It is absolutely amazing from an analytical standpoint. We (women) may ask a man a question, but we already have the answer in our minds. So, we are not really looking for *his* answer. We are merely looking for him to validate our own assumptions and perceptions. We don't really want to hear him. We just want a self centered validation. So, we ask him the question, and as soon as he opens his mouth to express how he feels, or more specifically, as soon as he says something that we don't agree with or believe, *that thing that deviates from our perception or assumption,* we jump right in and over-talk him either into submission to our will or into silence. When he submits, we win, or so we think. "Yeah! I knew it!" When he gets silent and refuses to either go on with the debate or concede, we get angry, not because he has given up, but because he refuses to submit. "Yeah I knew it! You don't even have to say it! Your silence says it all!" Or in the very rare case that we run into a man who is going to get his point across too- we get silent, shut down, and refuse to listen anymore. "If you're not gonna say it/admit it/tell the truth, there's no need to even have the discussion! I already know anyway."

And while many women who are privy to the former believe or embrace the power to "win an argument," the reality of it is that "winning an argument" in this manner- without reaching the goal of mutual understanding and resolution really isn't winning at all. And any woman who engages in this type of communication or conflict resolution style gains nothing in her perceived conquest. It is a detrimental and severely counterproductive pattern for two reasons. Communication is essential to the fiber of a relationship because it is only through communication that we find understanding and only through understanding that we can resolve conflict, reach a compromise, and commit each to the other. But more importantly, talking too damn much destroys our basic ability to <u>truly</u> hear what men think and feel, hence <u>truly</u> know who they <u>truly</u> are and how *they* <u>truly</u> feel-not how we feel about them, or how we think they feel. And how can you truly connect with someone that you really do not know? Answer: You can't.

The under current of this failure to listen, is that when it becomes excessive, and men do not feel heard or validated, when their needs are not being met in one form or another, because we did not listen and consequently don't know why, they will simply make quiet decisions about the interaction and relationship that we do not notice, and then they will drop the bomb that we weren't expecting, but should have noticed building the whole time. They walk away, break up with us, ask for divorce, cheat, or fail to commit-that is decide that we are not the ones to commit to. And we suddenly become the victim-when in actuality we were either perpetrators, co-conspirators, or at the least accomplices to our own heart break.

Are You His Michelle Obama?

Contrary to some of the assertions in Harvey's book, specifically his assertion that men will not be able to commit to a stable relationship until "his dreams have been or are being realized," I also found the contrary to be true. Harvey pointed out that although women tend to want to build, a man is not "gifted" enough to balance a relationship and build a career or pursue his goals at the same time. He states:

> "Many of you figure that if a man truly loves you, the two of you should be able to pursue your dreams together. Stability is important to you, but you'd rather build the foundation of your relationship together, no matter the man's station in life. This is honorable, but really, it's not the way men work. His eye will be on the prize, and that prize may not necessarily be you if he isn't up where he wants to be in life. It's impossible for us to focus on the two-we're just not that gifted."

This is what men said. One of the most common themes that came up in informal focus groups and discussions about love and commitment is reliability and the sense that "a woman has my back." Most men view this as a *core* characteristic across the board-from college students to middle aged divorcees and widowers.

Look at President Obama. In his speech, he gave "mad love" - *"I would not be standing here if it weren't for the unyielding love of my best friend for the last 16 years, the rock of our family and the love of my life- the next first lady Michelle Obama"* - to his *confidante, his best friend, the mother of his children*, to **his wife**- Michelle Obama. Why? Because, she "had his back!" She was his anchor while he was growing and pursuing his goals. He did not wait until he reached his goal (of political prominence) to marry her. In most power positions, especially political and social power positions (from the University to the Church)-being married is a precursor to opportunity and acceptance,

14

and hence a man's ability to reach that plateau anyway. Those who are truly in the "real game" know this fact. Most men are already married when they reach social and political power points. (I do not include those who acquire wealth through athletics and entertainment.) Obama realized and understood that she, Mrs. Obama (or even having a wife period) would be the core to his growth, progress, and success, and he committed- and the commitment wasn't out of favor to Mrs. Obama either, it was in his own best interest.

In essence, it is not that men do not want or cannot be in a relationship while they are growing in or building their careers, they just feel that if they are going to be in a relationship while they are building, they need to be in a stable relationship with a stable woman that will neither be a distraction or detraction from what they were trying to do, but a compliment and support for what they are trying to do and accomplish. Most men, especially older men, even argued that having a strong and complimentary woman by their side was essential to their success and achievements. The larger issue is simply grounded in their (men's) opinion that none were/are willing to deal with drama while building or pursuing goals and none are willing to risk "dealing" with a woman who does not fit in his plans. Consequently, if they even perceive that a relationship with "you" means drama and/or distraction or detraction, they'd rather not even take the chance.

The fact that support and strength were core characteristics of their ideal woman, the characteristics that distinguish "wifey" from "jump off," speaks volumes, and in some ways challenges Harvey's assertions. What it speaks to is the reality that when a man is ready, which is not only grounded in being financially stable or focused or on the way, he will be ready. When he "feels" a woman, "knows" that she is the one, he could be in a homeless shelter with no goals and he will commit to the one that he trusts and loves.

This concept extends from a phone call to a commitment. There is no such thing as being too busy. When a man is "feeling a woman," he will "make time"- period. He could be working 7 jobs, but if he is in love, he will spend his three hours sleeping in the woman he loves bed-just for the comfort of knowing he is near her, and the bed is hers. He will text while at work, call on his breaks, want to see her when he has time, and will consciously make time to see her-not because the woman nagged him to do so, or even asked him to- but because *he **wants*** to. (The operative words are "he" "wants" "to").

It's neither a man's or woman's nature to do or not to do that, it is basic *human* nature. It is a part of our human nature to "pursue" the human connections that we want and need because it gives us the necessary human feeling of belonging and connection, and allows us to use that energy to shape who we become. Human connection is essential, not optional. It is a core part of our basic human drive and existence. And I am not speaking about sexual connection alone, although that is a part. I am talking about the need to feel loved, supported, and cared for and about.

Not to invoke science, but we could look at that assertion from theoretical perspectives that range from the social psychological perspective (Maslow, Rogers, Mead, Erikson etc.), to developmental and criminological perspectives- looking at the influence of the lack of social contact/nurturing connection on the development of social, psychological, developmental, criminological problems. Not having adequate social interaction and connection can and does cause problems in human development and interaction. So, it is necessary. Therefore, even when a man is pursuing his dreams/goals, connection and support are still a necessary part of his process.

Therefore, "I don't have time," is most often just an excuse- not a lie- but a reason why a man cannot or does not want to commit, time-wise, relationship-wise, commitment-wise, marriage-wise- to that person that he does not have time for. They don't have time because they don't want or even feel the need or desire to make the time or commitment. Not maliciously- but just as a matter of fact, if a woman is not important to him- if she is simply not in his plans, just like any situation, she will be placed on the back burner for whatever reason. Again, there is nothing attached to the Y chromosome that renders a man unable to commit until he is either at the point or on his way to becoming the provider, that society tells him he should be. I don't even think Harvey waited until he was at the pinnacle of his career before marrying.

Being a provider is a social construct that is attached to the social characteristic of masculinity. And while it is important, being "there," arriving, or being on the way to being a provider is not an innate or gender focused precursor to commitment. This again can be proven in two forms, the many men who grow in their careers *within* their relationships and marriages (some notables are Samuel L. Jackson, Denzel Washington, and even youngster, Dwayne Wade-even though it did not turn out well). On the converse, one can analyze the men who fail to be providers *within* their relationships and marriages and still engage in relationships and marriages.

What Harvey didn't say, perhaps because he did not want to hurt our feelings is that when a man tells a woman (you) he doesn't have time for her (you), it is simply because (*that woman*) you *are not* the one that he is willing to "make time" for. It sounds harsh, but that is the simplest form of the truth. I delineate this for a very important reason, if a we walk away from that chapter in Harvey's work believing that he "is not ready" because he is "on his grind," we may feel compelled (as we often do) to wait (continue to pursue him) until he develops and accomplishes his goals-believing that he will be worth the wait, and will commit to us when he reaches his goal, when he has/had no intention of committing to us in the first place. And if we do so, we inadvertently become a part of a game that we cannot win. We make it comfortable for him by providing the temporary support that he needs until he finds "the one." And when he walks away from us or commits to another woman, we feel betrayed-used-abused.

I agree with Harvey's assertion in "mama's boy" when he states emphatically: "YES I SAID IT: IT"S YOUR FAULT." Preach, Steve and Deneen! It is our fault! But I think it's our fault for an entirely different reason. We part ways when Harvey asserts "a man who loves you will be the man *you need him to be* if *you* have requirements-standards you set to **make the relationship work the way you want it to**…" I would have ended the statement this way, "a man who loves you will be the man you need him to be…if you are the one he wants to be a man to." It's not about our requirements of *him*, it's about how well we fit into his model. That is the law of social exchange-mutual benefit and reward. And how well we fit his ideal is based on how well we know and understand self first and then him.

Men do not commit to and marry us because *we* set standards *for him*. We become more attractive energetically, when we have set standards for our "selves." They are not guided by all of the women in their lives, not even their mamas. Mothers set a part of the foundation for who their sons will become by/through the manner in which

18

they raise their sons. But, even before their sons become men, they define who they are and how they will live. Men are free thinkers, who, in relationships, are guided by the level of attraction (not just physical) to a woman.

That assertion only reinforces our flawed and often times selfish misperception of our influence and misunderstanding of men. Harvey goes on to state that "…if you don't have any standards or requirements, guess whose rules he's going to follow? That's right, his mother's." A mama may set the foundation and even serve as a model or an example of what a man wants his wife "to look like." But most men are not attached to their mothers breast and do not oscillate from mama to girlfriend/wife depending on who sets the best standards of manhood for him. I delineate this again because if we walk away from this assertion believing that we have to set requirements of/for him as "the man in our lives," that wives must compete with mothers and mothers must critique wives, and we do not have an idea of who we are and who he is, we cannot set requirements for who we must be in the context of a mutual relationship. If we embrace this "thinking," we leave Harvey's book with the same misperception of our role and power that we entered with.

Men were very clear. They want a woman who will have their backs as they grow. So, if he is growing and he does not embrace you, you are not the one, and you will probably never be the one that he makes the ultimate commitment to. That's the reason why when "he arrives" he marries her instead of you. It isn't that he changed. It isn't that you didn't set standards. It isn't even that his mother was better than you. It *is* because you were either never the one, or ceased looking like the one when you started setting your own 'groundless' and misguided requirements for his manhood.

The question for women then becomes, why are or aren't *you* "the one?" And the answer lies with you, not him. The self analysis involves examining whether you are a Queen or a Sapphire. In essence, can you be a Michelle Obama, or will you be an insecure, jealous, nagging, selfish, competitive, clingy, disrespectful dictator that will turn him off like a blown light bulb? Will you be so confined to your own ideals of what he is supposed to be doing and how that you fail to appreciate who he is? Or worse, will you be so caught up in your own agenda that you forget that the relationship and its outcome are *not* "just about you?"

Unfortunately many women are the latter-that is the insecure, jealous, nagging, selfish, competitive, clingy, disrespectful dictators that turn him off like a blown light bulb because we think *we* know what is best for *them,* and we don't know how to "play our position" or "know our role." Many of us, especially women who are more academically or financially advanced/stable/accomplished than their men and/or those of us who have come from generations of matriarchal families, have been trained to believe that *we* must culture, upgrade (lemme, lemme upgrade ya'), guide, protect, shape, mold, "make,"- or inevitably change or rather transform men into what we "think" they should be. But our efforts are severely strangled by the fact that we don't listen, and hence have NO IDEA of what and who we should be, much less who they should be.

Consequently, a relationship with many of us (including many of the co-dependent mothers- who think our son's are *our* husbands) would stifle a man's own growth, progress, goal orientation, aspirations, or more importantly- his "being" as not just a man, but a human "being."

So taking the chance of being with the dream reaper is simply not an option for many men- not because he can't balance, not because it's not in him, but because he *just* understands how truly counterproductive it would be-so he would never. It is simply not an option because it is not logical. Real men do not need a woman to define him-simply. So, those men who would undergo a relationship with the dream reaper most often do so out of their own lacking, insecurity, co-dependency, or necessity which will negatively manifest itself in the relationship or marriage anyway. He can engage with the dream reaper because he has no dreams. He can, or even must, engage with the control freak and allow a <u>wo</u>man to define his <u>man</u>hood because he does not know how to be a man or does not wish to take on his role as a real man. Think about it, what rational person would actively contribute to his, or even her, own derailment?

How many discussions have we (women) had about dating, or even being married to men who don't support *us?* We rally around that. We rally around bashing the emotional and psychological abusers who try to mold us, refuse to listen to us, refuse to honor, support, appreciate, or at the least understand our dreams. How about this, think about how stifled not only we feel, but think about the empathy that we feel for our ancestors who were stifled at the hands of patriarchal socio-political systems, communities, families and chauvinistic men where they were simply not allowed to pursue their dreams- had their dreams, goals, aspirations confined and limited by somebody else's perception of where women should be placed in society. So, what is the difference?

As we will discuss further in later chapters, we have to remember we will receive the energy that we emit. We will reap what we sow. So we have to plant our seed consciously, so that we can reap a fruitful harvest.

What Men Said About Love

In spite of my own heartbreaks, I never gave up on love, nor did I, or have I given up on men. I understood that it wasn't love that hurt me. Love wasn't wrong. It was the people that I chose to give my love to that were wrong for me, so I simply had to do a better job of choosing who I would give that gift to. I also never believed, nor do I believe, that all men are dogs. Nor have I ever believed that men are incapable of love. My belief and hope was reaffirmed and has consistently been reiterated by the conversations that I have had, but most recently by the focus groups and interviews that I had with "my young soldiers" at Virginia State University, and most importantly by conversing with and watching my own son.

On The Woman They Can Love

Respect, Intelligent, pretty, good communicator, independent (motivation to do something, not looking for somebody to do for them all the time), self respect, not fucking everybody, monogamous, faithful, trustworthy, goal oriented, strong morals, strong character, trustworthy, faithful, dependable, conscious, socially compatible, physical presence (attractive).

"Man she got to have substance. She gotta be somebody you can take home to Moms." "Yeah, yeah...you can't just take anybody home." "They gotta have self respect about em'. She can't just be no jump off." "Would you wife a jump off?" "Hell No!" "How do you know though? I mean sometimes you can't tell who's a jump off by just looking

at her." "True." "That's when the background check comes in handy. Gotta do your

homework." "Yeah you gotta do a background check, you gotta ask around campus,

check to see if she has a reputation, watch the girls she hangs with…" Almost

unanimously they all chime…"Awwww…her girls…." "Yeah the girls she hangs with

say a lot about her." "And you can tell by the way she carries it, being in a relationship

versus just lettin' a nigga hit." Underneath of the clamor, "More than likely if you got it

on the first night, so did somebody else." "But what if you just that good dude, and you

just got it like that?" "Yeah, just 'cause she like to fuck fast, don't mean she's a jump

off." "Depends on the situation, if y'all both drunk and then…" "Drink and fuck." They

all laugh. "Well if we both drunk, I'm not looking for a wifey." "You can't change

nobody cuz." "It can be done." "It won't last" "Yeah, the truth will come out." "It's just

some things you can't change." "I don't think you can use her girls as a guide because

like my girl, I love her and trust her but I hate her girls." "Yeah but, her girls tell a lot

about her, she ain't gonna hang with people she don't like. If she don't like what they

doing then…" "Yeah but that don't mean that she will do what they do." Division

occurs. "Naw, women just don't have friends, they don't even like each other. Jumps

travel in groups." "Yeah, there's a lot of competition between women." They all agree

again. "That's why you gotta have trust. I been with my girl for 8 years. She can go to

the club and I'm good. I can go and she know." "You can tell though, if she the one

looking for attention…"

How They Express Their Commitment

"I have that conversation." "I say it. I want to build. If she wants you then…" "Fuck assume." They all agree. *"Until you say the actual words, it is what it is."*

It was exceedingly clear. To the point, as they say, with "no chaser." Raw, uncut, unfiltered, unedited. This was their (own) conversation about love, commitment, and relationships. This is what men said.

Chapter 2
The Four States of Being

The very essence of society is contradictory unto itself. Society preaches non-violence and peaceful conflict resolution, yet we resolve our own conflicts through physical, verbal attack and war. Society preaches love, but it creates divisions- based on race, class, gender, religion, sexuality, political affiliation and on and on- that all promote divisiveness, intolerance, and even hate. Society preaches spirituality and religiosity and yet we are afraid to celebrate and publicly recognize religion and spirituality-as a part of our social and political spaces-possibly because the foundation of religion and its doctrines contradict so much of what we do socially and politically. Society preaches abstinence, piousness, purity, and the sanctity of monogamy and marriage, yet sex is the predominant marketing tool that is used to promote and sell everything from shampoo to cars. It is also the predominant weapon on radio, television and screen-from the development of reality shows that challenge stable relationships, to the internet to the strip club- all of which make money off of destroying the very sanctity of the values and institutions that are supposed to be a dominant part of our cultural institution. Given these sad realities, it becomes essential that we create, establish, and teach a more grounded and holistic understanding of all of these phenomena that we verbally say we want, desire, and strive for-love, trust, communication, conflict resolution, intimacy, commitment, and marriage.

As difficult as we make it- for whatever reason, the reality is that, in spite of the many self help seminars, self help books, and religious retreats and materials that we

25

spend billions on- establishing a beautiful, loving relationship is simple and free. It only involves conditioning and or re-conditioning our minds (collectively) around a very simple concept. *We are largely in control of our destiny through the decisions that we make.* PERIOD. If we understand *that* then we will work harder at cultivating healthy experiences and perceptions and/or changing our flawed perceptions about love, intimacy, relationships, and marriage, so that we can make better decisions.

It is a matter of first understanding who we are as individuals, as human beings- not as men over here, women over there- but as subjective beings who both require the same things and must not just co-exist but interact with one another in order to ensure the survival of our kind- even though we may take different paths toward getting to, and reaching that goal.

Where am I going with this? The vast majority of human beings are comprised of four states or parts of our being, or "self." These four states/parts/components of who we are cannot be compartmentalized and must, like any organism, be brought to balance and harmony in order for us to find inner peace and then harmony with our external environment. In essence we must bring balance to those four states so that we will be balanced as individuals, and subsequently be beautiful and positively attractive to others.

The four states of being are the physical state of being, the emotional state of being, the mental state of being, and the spiritual state of being. This concept is grounded in philosophies that go back to the great Kemetic philosophies and principles of existence, and have traveled over and through time to modern day theorists, philosophers, and religious and spiritual leaders. The *physical* state of being is the lowest, most basic, yet the most essential state of being on many levels. If one were to compare it to

Maslow's Hierarchy of Needs Chart, the essentiality of the physical state of being corresponds to a human's fundamental biological and/or physiological needs. It encompasses the need for water, food, shelter, clothing (which represents protection of the body). However, when the other states are not properly developed and functional, the physical state of being reflects a human's basic existence. It reflects a human's superficial or physical relationship with his environment that is only based on what and/or how he can use the environment to satisfy his physical needs. Although some would ask why sex wasn't included, it is argued that sex is a desire that is coupled with the emotional and rational components of man. It does not dictate the survival of the individual and is not an essential part of an individual's biological function. To include sex in this category would be to support, what I argue are erroneous assumptions that the sexual drive of humans mimics that of lower animals who strictly use sex (mating) to procreate through physical means (such as fanning, emitting pheromones etc.) without any emotional or intimate/pleasure seeking attachments or drives associated with it.

When an individual is driven by his "lower state," he does not have the capacity to look at anything, much less anyone outside of how that thing or person can be used to satisfy his most basic needs. In the context of society then, what becomes important is survival and he will do anything that he "feels" he needs to do to survive-just like an animal does. As Freud would argue, the physical without regulations functions as the id does. That is it is uninhibited without the regulation of the higher states of being that causes the individual to pursue his physical needs within socially acceptable confines.

In the scientific world, it is argued that human beings are different from animals because unlike animals, human beings have the capacity for thought, logic, and

27

consciousness. They function at a higher level. Therefore, society is able to impose laws, boundaries, values, etc. that govern and guide individuals so that order and conformity are maintained. This scientific premise comes from the assertion being presented here. Being able to operate at a higher level involves a human's capacity to nurture their mental and spiritual components, and then to use those states to balance and guide their interaction with their environment.

When an individual is operating on the physical, or when the physical consumes the larger part of an individuals being, he will act like an animal. When hungry, he will do whatever it takes to eat-steal, kill.. When thirsty, he will do whatever it takes to drink. When he needs shelter, he will do whatever it takes to find and secure it. When he is consumed by lust or material gain, he will do whatever it takes to satisfy it-rape, kill. This is true of the man who has a girlfriend and cannot say no to the advances of a "jump off" or the woman who needs the bills paid, and is willing to give her body to get the money, or even an inmate who would rather compromise his sexual orientation to satisfy himself than to wait. Like an animal, it will not matter who he hurts in his process, it will be all about him/her-either because he knows nothing else, or he has not developed the capacity through nurturing his higher states, to care.

As a result, anyone who interacts with this person will be unfulfilled because that person is incapable of feeling anyone outside of himself. In relationships then, he (or she) will manifest the characteristics of the selfish, narcissistic user. And even though, in this person's mind, he/she may feel that they are "on point" because they are able to get their needs met, the detriment is to their own selves. Why? Because, they will go through life skating on superficial interactions that leave the inner self under or undeveloped and unfulfilled.

The second state of being is the ***emotional***. The emotional state of being is the state that is, as the term suggests, guided by emotion- that is our body's mental reactions to our external experiences. The emotions include joy, sorrow, anger, love (as a feeling), passion, hate, jealousy, envy, aggression and on and on. The catch is that while emotions are a normal part of our mental process, the way that we express emotion is most often physical. When we are happy we smile. When we love, we hug or verbally express, when we are angry we "lash out." Consequently and in addition to that how we develop our emotions is based on our experiences, and how we express our emotion will be guided by how we develop our states of being.

Feeling and expressing our emotions is a natural part of our being. Coupled with a healthy balance and integration of the four states of being, feeling and expressing emotion can be a beautiful reflection of who we are. However, without the balance and guidance of the mental and spiritual, invoking the emotional into, or coupling it with the physical, and vice versa, can be a lethal combination. Every murder, suicide, fight, ill word, bad deed, busted window, slashed tire, bleached shirt, or even every one night stand or alcohol binge can be attributed to this combination. Every impulsive action that was guided by emotion falls into this category.

I'm feeling her/him, he/she is fly, I'm gonna hit that-combination of emotional and physical. That mutha… made me mad, so I hit him-combination of emotional and physical. I wasn't planning on doing it to him/her, but it was the heat of the moment-

29

combination of the emotional and physical. Or on the converse how about, I didn't like him, but the sex was good-I think I'm in love-combination of emotional and physical.

The emotional and physical are often accomplices in the most destructive decision making. They find comfort in and instigate one another. But they are still the two lowest states that do not separate us from animals. Even animals feel emotion. They feel threatened by humans they scratch, bite, and even kill. When they smell the pheromones of other animals, they mate. When they are jealous or feel threatened by another animal threatening their territory, they fight and kill. They are not able to process their emotions, nor are they able to make rational decisions about them. This is what separates humans from lower animals.

When their territory is confronted by another, they are not able to gauge the other animal's intentions or agenda rationally. There is no rationality to it. It is strictly a physical gauge. Animals are not able to sit down and rationally discuss problems and resolve conflict. Physical displays, submission, fighting, and the death of one is the resolution. Lower animals do not date, fall in love, marry and decide to have children. Mating is an innate part of their being and is governed by the onset of physical/biological manifestations that send signals that it is time-mating season or mating time. The emotion of animals is guided not by rationality and thought, but merely through physical experience and interaction. Therefore, as harsh as it may sound, humans who resist, fail, or refuse to develop their higher states of being, fail to develop their own capacity to govern themselves and their interaction with their environment and go through life in the same manner as lower animals.

The third state of being is the ***mental***. This is the transition or perhaps the bridge to the higher state of being and interacting. But, unlike the emotional and physical, the mental state must be cultivated and nourished consciously and through our social experiences. This state of being is parallel to Freud's concept of the super-ego. It is the part of the self that must be nurtured through our interaction with our external environment, through our establishment, processing and understanding of the values, norms, expectations, laws, knowledge that will guide who we will become. Of course we are products of our experiences, but…how we process our experiences, hence how we interact will be determined by how we develop our mental state of being.

The mental state is cultivated by the acquisition of knowledge-and then internalizing the knowledge gained from many sources so that we transform that knowledge into wisdom- and finding the meaning or understanding-not only of what we experience, but of who we are. The more deeply we do this, the more conscious we become. The greater the level of consciousness, that is our ability to analyze and process on deeper levels than just the superficial, the stronger the bridge to the spiritual becomes.

Many people today minimize the mental from an intellectual and a consciousness standpoint. People do not want to listen, they do not want to open their minds to new information/knowledge, they don't want to go to school or pay attention in class, they don't want to read or work to nourish their minds and stimulate and develop their brains, they don't want to think too hard or be challenged mentally or intellectually-challenged to think critically as opposed to being spoon fed others interpretations of information and experiences. Therefore, they fail to truly develop the individual sense of self, that many think they have but do not, and in such end up being "puppets" that are controlled by forces outside of them "selves."

The mental is not just shaped by formal means of education though. For formal means of education, especially primary and secondary educational systems are designed more-so to teach the basics that will instill a common knowledge (language, mathematics, history and social studies) that allows humans to communicate and interact on the same level, and then promote a system where all are internalizing a universal ideology, and learning conformity. The mental is also shaped by our experiences- those external situations and environments that we find ourselves in that ultimately become a part of who we are and shape how we perceive. And so, we have to be mindful of how we nourish ourselves. We have to be mindful of what we either indirectly or directly feed our "selves" by and through the situations, experiences, and environments that we place ourselves in.

My mother once told me. "You are what you eat. If you eat shit you are shit." If you eat shit, you will be shit. If you are listening to shit, you will allow that shit to either consciously or unconsciously become a part of your being. If you are watching shit, you will allow that shit to either consciously or unconsciously become a part of your being. If you are reading shit, you will…well you get the message. Because of the nature of the human body, specifically the relationship between the senses and the brain, everything that we see, hear, smell, and taste shapes and becomes a part of our experience. Because of the intricate nature of receiving, processing, decoding, and then understanding or assigning meaning to the sensory information that is received, our brains naturally store those stimuli or those experiences. Those things, therefore, become a part of who we are.

The information that is stored then shapes how we perceive as we recall or draw from it in order to assign meaning to new experiences and/or stimuli.

Let me give two examples of this process. We learn the word "banana" young. Now even reading the word here in this book, which is not about "bananas" will invoke a recall a subconscious picture that gives understanding of what it really is, what the word really means. This is because as we learn to read, the letters and words are most often accompanied by a picture. Oftentimes the words are words that we already know by association. So through the educational process, we learn that it is a fruit and see that it is long and yellow. Then we learn that the banana is spelled-b.a.n.a.n.a. That is the formal educational part of our mental development or conditioning. Through our experience then we have touched, smelled, and tasted. This sensory experience allows us to more deeply understand the makeup of the banana. It is thick on the outside covered by a peel that we must "peel off" to get to the fruit on the inside. It is squishy. It tastes fibrous and sweet and it is mushy or even slimy in the mouth. It smells sweet. This information is stored in the brain. When you see another banana, recall allows us to understand what it is and rehash our sensory experiences. When we see the word we rehash our sensory experiences. If we eat a banana flavored now n later, or a banana cake, the consistency is not the same, but our brain remembers that the "banana" taste is banana. Although it may seem so, this process is not automatic. It is the result of the interaction between our sensory experiences and our brain/mental processing.

Example two, Jane is at the park alone on a lovely evening looking at the stars. The park is a beautiful park with a beautiful lake, trees, and flowers. When she is leaving she is attacked and mugged by three girls. Tom proposes to Mary at the same park in the same spot that Jane was mugged. These are two completely different experiences in that same external environment. The experience will shape Jane, Tom, and Mary's perception of that park and that spot. Recall. The memories that Jane has will invoke an entirely different perception of that park and that space-that perception will invoke an entirely different emotion and reaction than Mary and Tom. While Tom and Mary may frequent that park and feel feelings of love and connection, based on Mary's experience it is unlikely that she would return, and if she did, it is unlikely that she would be free from any negative feelings.

The mental is the state of being that brings rationality, logic, and thought to an individual. It is the conscious state of processing information and, in essence, guiding our decision making, interaction etc. In Freud's concept of the conflict between the id and the superego, the physical would represent the id and the mental would represent the super ego. The mental is the component that will or should ultimately guide the physical and the emotional. When the mental is developed adequately and occupies a balanced part of an individual's sense of self, it will adequately govern our emotions and our physical being. However, when it is not adequately developed it will allow, encourage, protect, and rationalize our misguided actions, decisions, and interactions. That is why it is so important to grow mentally, to nurture ourselves mentally-so that we will be more prepared to make decisions that are truly in our best interest and will promote the types of relationships and lives that we say we want to live.

The *spiritual* is the highest and most precious, significant, and important state of being. I am going to take my time on elaborating on the spiritual because it is a component of self that, if nourished and depended upon, can produce a highly rewarding

34

life experience that most people never have in their life times. This is so because most people are guided by the lower three levels and fail, even in their churchgoing, gospel choir singing, bible-toting, or highly intellectual and materially successful lives to really understand what the concept of "spirituality" really entails.

I emphasize the later part of that paragraph not as a means to demean those who may be religious, but to underscore that being religious, is different from being spiritual. This may offend some, even many, but I must be clear. There are many people who feed themselves in the church and are being fed by the pastor, imam, priest- instead of being fed by the will and word of God (in all translations of His name)-The Creator, The Most High. They run to church on Sundays and Holidays, they read the passages of the bible, they hang on every word of the pastor, they pray (most often when life is posing some form of challenge), dance and even speak in tongues, and they preach and minister to others- and they believe that those deeds form their relationship with God, Allah, Jehovah, or their Higher Power. But, in it all, they fail to understand what it really means. They fail to integrate those things into guiding their entire being. This section may go over the heads of many, but here it goes.

The spiritual is the part of the "self" that is nourished and _**guided**_ by a Higher Power. I have to repeat that. The spiritual is the part of the "self" that is nourished and guided by a Higher Power. It is the part of the self that understands that there is some One and/or some Energy "greater than the self" that must guide and shape our lives here on Earth, to whom and to which we must be accountable. Our accountability to this being must guide our lives, when it becomes optional and where we deviate is the challenge. It is the part of the self that realizes that our deeds in this life will have consequences on many levels-not just physical consequences, but spiritual consequences. And in such it forces the individual to recognize that there must be a sense of accountability not just to one's self and one's own needs or even the needs of those around him/her, or close to her, but to the universe. It is the force that helps us to not only realize but live our lives committed to and guided by the belief that one must not only be accountable to "this" life and "this" world, but his deeds will also make him accountable at higher levels- during and after this life. It is that internal connection to the Higher Power that could ideally create a utopian world.

What does this mean? We have all heard and told stories of the one who goes to church and puts on "a front" for the pastor, congregation, and even God- the one who lives for the church and "spits" religion at every turn, but has an 'evil' attitude- a mean, hateful, selfish, or detached disposition. I am speaking of the one that chases religion, not to get closer to God or to hear the message so that it can be used to shape his/her life, but the one who chases religion to either justify his/her judgmental nature, make him/herself look or feel bigger or better, or most commonly to bail her/him self out of the problems that his lack of connection to the will of God, has and continues to cause in the first place.

We have all heard or experienced times when things were going great in our lives and we forgot that God-or our Higher Power-even existed. We got a raise because *we* worked our asses off, we had that healthy baby because *we* labored for 16 hours and ate right during our pregnancy or he has that master sperm, we got that man because *we* looked good, we look good because of our *Daddy's* genes, we bought that new car or house because *we* saved, we missed that accident because *we* were good drivers….But, then as soon as a challenge, obstacle, or God forbid some eye awakening problem or tragedy occurs- we are the first to open our address book so that we can call on God.

We make up our own minds about what we want to do and how we want to live our lives without consulting or relying on God's guidance. We make decisions about minor and major things using our lowest three levels consistently, forgetting that God is even or at least should be guiding us every single day. And then when shit goes wrong we want to either blame God or call him up so that he can bail us out-help us to make the decisions we made without his consultation beneficial, help us ease the pain from our decisions, or bail us out of the consequences of our decisions. Think about it! It is really hilariously illogical. You knew he/she was a jerk, but you married him/her anyway, and then when the marriage is falling to shit, you call on God. Well if you had listened to God (The Higher Power) in the first place and let Him (it) guide you, you wouldn't be in that predicament. If you had allowed God (A Higher Power, the spiritual as opposed to the physical) guide you, you would have set your wants aside and understood that "these things" were very clear signs that "that place" was not where God, or the Universe, or your own Spiritual senses wanted or needed you to go, or where they needed you to be. And even though having to deny that course may have caused minor physical and/or emotional discomfort, you would have seen that the reward waiting was far greater, or at the least, you would have avoided the deeper conflict, disappointment, or pain. Do you understand the depth of that?

When one is guided by the spiritual, he/she will understand that there is so much in the world that is greater than the self. In such, we will be able to appreciate "life"- simply. Not a superficial appreciation, but a deep seeded appreciation for the things that we so often overlook in our daily grinds or the pursuit of superficial, material, or immaterial things. Money won't mean as much- because, we will understand that it is JUST a social construct that is a means to an end- a piece of paper that has no more worth than what the government assigns it in that day. So we will not covet it, but will use it for good.

Instead, we will wake up in the morning and be thankful for the sun, snow, blue sky, rain, daffodils, and our loved ones. We will be thankful for the many blessings that we can all count, instead of harping on the things that we don't. We will do good in and with our lives so that we will be truly favored in the eyes of the Most High…and in such we will find that the rewards that we receive in this life and after are far greater than that Benz with a car note…that 700,000 dollar home with three more rooms than we need…that handsome well endowed man who endows everyone else but us. It's not just tithing to the church or to the pastor, it is a life tithe that comes out of our commitment to seeking and fulfilling our divine purposes that leads to happiness that is bestowed by The Most High and brings us infinite peace and happiness.

I know this may sound corny to most because it is an existence that most could never even conceptualize, much less reach. Not because they can't, but because they refuse to nurture the spiritual side that will make this type of existence and interaction a reality in their own lives. Imagine a life where we don't stress about getting that flat screen TV because we have one and our cable bill is paid-not that we shouldn't strive to get the material things that we want, but they don't run us. Imagine if we were so content with our inner selves that it didn't matter if we had a significant other or not- not that we shouldn't desire a beautiful relationship- because as I stated, connection is essential; but, finding or searching or waiting for it doesn't consume us. If those things could be, we could be genuinely happy for our friends that got the flat screen before we did. We could go to the club and have fun without gauging or defining our fun based on how many numbers we got. We could go to our friends wedding and truly be happy for them-not be jealous, or worse envious. We could ride in *our partners new car and not wish we had it, kill someone or ourselves to get it, risk our* futures, destroy and negate our morality etc, to try to get it or try to "out-do" them.

Then imagine if two people who were on the same plane connected. POWER! They would first connect on the spiritual plane and that spiritual connection would drive the mental/intellectual connection, and then the love (emotion) would grow out of that connection. Imagine how powerful that love making session would be! It would be powerful because the physical connection would be an expression of all of the other connections, all of the things that each feels for the other. There would be no issues because the trust and love would be there, so the physical and/or intimate connection would be a manifestation of all of those things. Can you imagine?

When one is guided by the spiritual, his/her decisions, hence his/her life will be guided by something greater than the self. That person will understand that if he/she has to be accountable to a Higher Power, in every deed, and that every deed will have a consequence-be it positive or negative-he/she will be more selective in how he lives. That person will understand that if s/he wants his/her experiences, hence his or her life, to be a positive one, then he/she must live a positive life that is guided by making righteous and often times self-less, instead of selfish, decisions.

You cannot encourage cheating by being the chick on the side or "boyfriend number 2" and think that *that* relationship, or the one that you are really into is going to turn out beautiful- it won't-EVER. You can't be a liar and expect that those around you are going to be truthful to you. You can't steal and think that what you have stolen is going to be profitable or stable. You can't breed confusion and negativity in your life or the lives of others and think that you are going to have peace. The adage "you reap what you sow is not just a fluke." The adage "karma is a bitch" isn't just a saying, its real. She (karma) can be as beautiful as the sun, and as angry as the tornado. She will manifest what you give 10 to 100 fold. If you manifest beautiful, she will give you beautiful. But, if you manifest ugly-she will wreak havoc…and it may not be an immediate response. But nothing ugly stays beautiful forever.

When one embraces his/her spiritual energy he/she will understand that the law of the harvest exemplifies the law of human energy and deed. The seed that one plants in the earth dictates what he will grow. If one plants a corn seed, he will grow corn. If one plants an apple seed, then he will grow an apple tree. If one has an apple tree then he will reap apples. One will never reap cherries from an apple tree. So we are, and the lives we create- will be, dictated by the deeds that we do, the seeds that we, ourselves, plant in our own lives. Therefore, as we will discuss later, and as India Arie points out in her son, "if we want a butterfly, we have to be a butterfly."

Chapter 3
What Women Feel

There is a concrete contradiction between what women feel and how women act that becomes more pronounced when it is compounded by the different experiences that women have based on the intersection of their gender and race, class, religion, nationality, ethnicity, family background, and/or cultural affiliation etc. Even in theory, it is acknowledged that women share very different experiences based on not only those intersecting factors, but also by the woman's historical relationship with society.

Many books, articles, studies attempt to lump all women into this homogenous grouping, and many gender studies works assume that all women subscribe to and have been privy to traditional Western gender role values, characteristics, and privileges-and have hence encountered problems as women at the same level. However, even historically, most women have not been privy to being able to completely assume the traditional gender role values, characteristics, and privileges due to her relationship with society.

First, what are the traditional gender role characteristics? The "cult of true womanhood"- which is based on 18th and 19th century European values states that a woman is supposed to be "pious, pure, submissive, and domestic"- goes along with the assigned socio political position that women have been given in patriarchal societies-nurturer. In these patriarchal societies, her predominant and most important social and familial roles of *wife and mother*, and her social construction of nurturer required that she embrace these socially defined gender role characteristics. In examining each of the attributes defined in the "cult of true womanhood," they correspond to some very specific patriarchal values.

Piousness, which involves having a "reverence," or a high degree of respect for hence fear of God, is essential to ensuring that a woman be "a good" woman-one who was guided by her religious values and virtue. This concept relates to the spiritual component of the self (in spite of the fact that it is often misinterpreted by men and power structures who attempt to use it to oppress and subjugate women). It means that (as will be discussed later) if a woman has reverence and fear for God, she will conduct herself by the religious principles that include no fornication or adultery. This means that the men in society can be confident that she will be pure for him.

Purity simply means being "pure" sexually-a virgin, keeping her body and womb "in tact" for her husband-who will be her first. These two characteristics work together to ensure that a woman remains a virgin and "keeps herself faithful to God" until she is "given" to her husband, and then keeps herself faithful to her husband through God until she is given back to God. While many may analyze this on a superficial sexual level, given the historic nature of patriarchal systems it is a logical patriarchal value. Let me explain this assumption.

Staying pure and committed to ones husband sexually becomes especially relevant when it comes to bearing children. It is essential because in an era where men were traditionally the predominant caretakers/providers of/for the family, and in an era where the inheritance was to be passed on to the male heirs, it was essential that a man's offspring and heirs actually be his own. So, the way to ensure that those values were instilled and maintained was to implement them into the social, political, and cultural spheres of society and ensure that the social constructions of womanhood- that encouraged women to adhere to the principles of abstinence, monogamy, and overall sexual virtue-became a core part of the socialization process.

Submissiveness, involves a woman being submissive or passive to her man. That means not challenging or attempting to regulate him, but instead acquiescing to and/or honoring his will, next to the will of God. This ensures that men will be the dominant forces and decision makers in the household, that the husband/father will control his home and his family, and remain the example of "strength" in the community and what it takes to be successful, and even dominant in the workforce and in society. In such, all women would operate through the will of a man, be it her father or husband.

And *domesticity,* speaks for itself. It is being domestic, taking care of the home and all that home encompasses-cooking, cleaning, caring for the children etc. Although today, the very essence of the "cult of true womanhood" probably makes most women cringe, it had a very distinct purpose and worked in a complimentary sense to promote the health of the family in the 17th and 18th centuries when it was constructed.

In patriarchal societies-and in middle class families- where the women were nurtures and men were providers, the gender role characteristics that were associated with those two roles worked to ensure that each gender would be socialized to fulfill those roles. For example, if we were to analyze the gender role characteristics presented in the literature on gender roles and gender role characteristics (from Introduction to Sociology texts to feminist theory books), we would find that some common characteristics associated with gender are as follows. Men: strong, assertive, aggressive, competitive, rational, dominant- "thinking". Women: weak, passive, nurturing, emotional, submissive- "feeling".

These are completely opposite roles, but very complimentary-if the dials are aligned in the right position. Two of the same often poses conflict, so in this case, as they state—opposites work out fine. In essence, the characteristics associated with men are necessary to protect and provide for his family. In the work force, men must leave the confines of home and compete in the world to provide (financially) for his family, according to tradition. Therefore, he must be strong. He must be assertive and competitive. He must think rationally and must not be consumed by emotion-which is thought to be a distraction to rational functioning and decision making. He must be direct in his approach and without obvious "weaknesses" or gaps that can be exploited by other men who are competing with him for resources. Still today it is asserted that those "feminine characteristics" have no place in the "world"- in the world- in the "cut throat" division of labor.

On the converse, the gender role characteristics of a woman are essential to her being able to nurture and provide emotional support to and for her family-husband and children. Nurturing is being able to connect to and take care of the emotional needs, ensure the emotional well being of her family. Therefore, she must be able to use her emotional and feeling side- now known as that infamous-*maternal instinct*- to do that. If she is in the home, she is responsible, not only for the domestic duties; but, she is also responsible for supporting her husband by not being- or presenting- conflict in the home, by giving him the emotional support that he needs to process the daily grind rationally. "How was your day dear? Awww…it was stressful, here let me fix you a cup of tea and

rub your back while you tell me about it...Well I know you'll handle it in the morning."
You see, it involves providing the emotional space and letting him process-without
invoking our opinions of how we think he should handle the situation-after all, how could
we know?

If he is to go out and deal with the world (even when women must as well), his
home must be his peace-and it is up to the wife to ensure that it is so. That is the social
definition of a good wife. It doesn't matter if the husband contributes to or even causes
household chaos, it is the woman's responsibility to fix it and if she can't it is only a
reflection of her ability to handle her role as a wife and mother. And even today, most
women still adhere to that socially constructed value. Therefore, in this patriarchal
relationship, she must be passive to his aggressive, emotional to his rational, let him take
the "lead" so that he will serve as an example of what his son's are supposed to be as men
and his daughters are supposed to expect from their husbands.

This is how the traditional gender role characteristics work and why they were
established. May seem strange to many now because as the productive forces, and the
economy has changed and evolved so have the social responsibilities and roles of men
and women. In an era where women, specifically European middle class women could
not/were not allowed and expected to work (and if they did reflected poorly on a man),
this relationship was a complimentary and mutually interdependent relationship.
However, much of the literature fails to acknowledge that this role and privilege was
dramatically absent for working class and poor families, which in the U.S includes
Eastern European immigrant women, and especially African American women.

Historically, many women were not privy to this status because during the industrial revolution, post emancipation, and during the expansionist wars, they too had to work to help provide for their families-whether it was on the books wage labor or not. As Sojourner Truth illustrated in her speech *"Ain't I A Woman,"* African American women were much more significantly denied the assignment of the characteristics and social privileges of "a woman" as the result of not only enslavement, but as a result of the social, political, and economic disenfranchisement that African American men faced post Emancipation. Although many African American women worked without pay, and were not a part of the labor force during the initial stages after Emancipation, the still worked well into the domestic era. However, even though they were not given the status and social privilege of "womanhood," it did not stop them from being forced to compete with the label and define, question, or defend why they were not privy to the protection and privilege that came with "womanhood" during that era. They still had to work hard to dispel the myth of their objectivity and biological inferiority.

"That man over there says that women need to be helped into carriages, and lifted over ditches, and to have the best place everywhere. Nobody ever helps me into carriages, or over mud-puddles, or gives me any best place! And ain't I a woman? Look at me! Look at my arm! I have ploughed and planted, and gathered into barns, and no man could head me! And ain't I a woman? I could work as much and eat as much as a man - when I could get it - and bear the lash as well! And ain't I a woman? I have borne thirteen children, and seen most all sold off to slavery, and when I cried out with my mother's grief, none but Jesus heard me! And ain't I a woman?

Then they talk about this thing in the head; what's this they call it? [member of audience whispers, "intellect"] That's it, honey. What's that got to do with women's rights or negroes' rights? If my cup won't hold but a pint, and yours holds a quart, wouldn't you be mean not to let me have my little half measure full?

Then that little man in black there, he says women can't have as much rights as men, 'cause Christ wasn't a woman! Where did your Christ come from? Where did your Christ come from? From God and a woman! Man had nothing to do with Him.

If the first woman God ever made was strong enough to turn the world upside down all alone, these women together ought to be able to turn it back , and get it right side up again! And now they is asking to do it, the men better let them. " (Sojourner Truth, 1851)

In essence, society did not redefine the "cult of true womanhood" or recognize that all women did not experience womanhood at the same intersection, hence create a more inclusive definition or more inclusive characteristics. But, instead created, as Collins (2004) termed "a binary construction" of womanhood where those who did not fit the traditional mold were/are considered abnormal-or denied their subjective and social privileges as women. Consequently then, society did not create a different means of socializing men and women who did not fit the traditional role. Those men and women were (and still are) forced to balance the contradiction of what they are and what they are supposed to be-in spite of the fact that society has not and does not give all equal opportunity to assume those roles. While different men and women may interact with his/her social environment at different locations, all are still uniformly conditioned and socialized, which leads to the point of this chapter.

Because of the social roles of women, baby girls are socialized from the uterus to "be women" to internalize these "feminine roles and values." While many may still argue gender is innate, that there are characteristics associated attached to the X and Y chromosome that make boys and girls, men and women act the way that they do, I argue that it is completely learned. However, because it is an innate part of our societal socialization process, it mimics being innate to our biological makeup.

What does this mean? Think about it. There are actions and materials associated with masculinity and femininity. These actions and materials are assigned from the

47

moment parents find out the sex of their fetus. "Oh, I'm having a girl." The baby shower is adorned with pink and the gifts are all "gender appropriate" gifts-that is gifts that are traditionally associated with girls. Pink dresses, frilly socks and tights, stuffed bears, barrettes and ribbons etc. When she is old enough to start playing with toys, the toys are all toys that predominantly relate to her role as mother and wife- from shopping carts, bubble vacuum cleaners, easy bake ovens, ballerina slippers, make up kits, high heeled shoes, and doll babies that "pee pee," eat, burp, cry, spit up and even poop. Although this has changed dramatically since the feminist revolution and Title IX, when she is old enough to participate in activities, she is placed in activities like dance and cheerleading. The chores she is assigned are domestic chores such as dishes, vacuuming-in-house chores-especially if she has a brother. When she falls or hurts herself, she is coddled and expected to process and receive support for her feelings. We never smack her on the butt and tell her shake it off. She is further traditionally trained to be a lady, to be discreet, quiet, naïve even- even when she is doing dirt. Everyone doesn't have to know the business, act like a lady.

So by the very nature of the socialization process, girls are trained to take on their roles as mothers and wives from a very young age. They are trained to "get in touch" with their femininity and are nurtured through developing that emotional side that is often ridiculed. When she is tough as a child, she is labeled a "tom-boy" or a "butch." When she is "out of character" she is ridiculed for acting like a man. And as a woman, when she takes on roles that are traditionally "reserved" for men, she is labeled a bitch. When she is not married with children by the age of 30, she is labeled a "spinster." When she is not the primary caretaker of her children, she is labeled "a bad mother."

48

In every fairy tale, she is taught that being the damsel in distress, waiting for her prince charming to save her so that she can get married and live happily every after defines her very essence as a woman. And no matter how much women may try to deny it, much of what we do is guided by this socialization process-most often because we know no different. It doesn't matter how *we* feel about ourselves as women, what matters more is how others see us. I may be a damn good mother, but I don't want to be absent at too many games, while my husband is present, because I don't want the other soccer moms to notice that I'm never there. Why? Because I don't want to be perceived, by others, as a bad mom-no matter what I know and how I feel about myself.

When I go out, while I'd like to think I want to dress for myself, I dress in a manner that I believe will encourage the response of others. Predominantly, if I am "looking for the attention" I am going to dress in a manner that will garner attention-and what I wear will be determined by "what type of attention" I want to get-what type of image I want to present, and "what type of attention" I want to get will be determined by how I have assessed "the game."

The point I am trying to make is that women are trained to feel. We are trained to desire love, marriage, and family-not because we always feel that *that* is best, but because women are *socially* defined by whether we accomplish the goal of wife and mother or not. We can take Oprah as a prime example. More women have a hard time with Oprah's womanhood and femininity than men do. As successful as she is as a woman, women still feel that she is "missing something"-that she is not a well-rounded "woman" because she has not married and does not have children. And when women try to justify the perceived imbalance in Oprah's life, we sip coffee and find acceptance in the agreement that she sacrificed family, (hence an integral part of her womanhood and femininity), to be successful (in the masculine part-career). The very nature of the discussion is a testament to the fact that although many of us would like to believe that we are not conformists-that we support "success" that is not confined to/by patriarchal values, we are all sucked in to the same ideals of womanhood that places the role of wife and mother above all else. The very nature of the fact that we cannot, or blatantly refuse to, believe that a woman can be happy with her "self" as a woman when she does not have the traditional family, is a testament to how deeply engrained the social virtues of womanhood have been rooted into our own souls and beings.

Even when women assert that they do not want or need a family, there has to be something wrong. How many times have I heard, "Oh, Stedman must not want to marry her." "Why wouldn't Oprah have children, she has so much to offer?" "Is Stedman just a cover up for her lesbianism?" We do this, because as women, we are trained to believe that *we* are not complete unless we have fulfilled our gender roles as wife and mother, or at least, mother. If Oprah were a man, there would be no problem with her decision not to marry or have a family. It would not be because a woman didn't want her/him, s/he would not be considered selfish. It would not be abnormal because it is not the social expectation of men.

There was even criticism of Halle Berry too. As beautiful and successful as she is, she did not complete her womanhood, in the eyes of many, until she married and then later had her daughter. So, those women who choose not to adhere to traditional gender role values---are labeled lesbian, bitch, and/or even failures.

While this assertion may seem minimal, it has two very real implications. The first implication is the reality that the acceptance of this assignment is frequently at the root of: dysfunctional relationships and marriages, decisions to remain in unhappy, unfulfilling relationships and marriages instead of being at peace single, the disenchantment of valuing our own solitude and independence over chasing a relationship, the countless numbers of loved children who are born out of wedlock as an exception or a "settle" to marriage and traditional family and even our failure to define our womanhood in heterogeneous and subjective ways as opposed to just believing that the societal and patriarchal definition must be it. In such, many women end up wasting much time on a pursuit of happiness that will never come, because we have failed to first

ir own happiness and inner peace, and are searching for someone to "make us

nd implication is the core of this chapter. In being disappointed by our

relationships with our fathers, significant male figures in our lives,

ps and/or marriages- instead of changing how we feel about our *selves*,

ding that our womanhood is NOT and must NOT be defined by whether or not, or how fast we become wives and mothers, but how we go about becoming wives and mothers and/or fulfilling our other subjective and personal goals (whether being a wife and motherhood is a part of our goals or not), we alter our routes, change the path of how we reach the same goal. But we erroneously do so by trying to fool ourselves into believing that we do not desire the same goal, that we can escape attachment to our socialization and the fairy tales of happily ever after's that we are taught and read about.

It is clear that the sexual revolution and feminist liberation facade has taken over-made women feel more free about flexing their independence, sexual freedom, ability to pursue professions/jobs that were traditionally reserved for men, compete with men, be just as, if not more successful than men, go to the same schools, play the same sports and on and on. But, most still want to be married. And most women still want to be in monogamous relationships while they are dating. Most want to feel loved and respected by their men. Most want to be "treated like a lady." Most want and expect to be protected. And the fallacy-and escape hatch of "gold digging" aside, most women want and expect to be provided for and protected-even if they are also contributing to the household.

This assertion is evidenced by the problems that couples across race and class lines experience when women take on traditionally masculine roles, such as being the provider or worse, the protector in her household. Or more specifically, it is evidenced in the disrespect and disdain that women often express toward the men that they 'feel' they are "carrying," or "taking care of" and the relationships and marriages that they 'feel' they are carrying the weight and/or the burden of. This is because it is expected that, even when a woman is working, her income and contribution will be secondary and/or supplemental. It is expected that the man will earn more than she does, and the bulk of the financial responsibility will be carried by him. And the closer she is to carrying half of the weight, the trickier the relationship dynamics get.

This is because reversing roles challenges the traditional assertions of femininity and masculinity. When those roles begin to cross, the predominant question women ask is "what good are you?" In essence, she and her girlfriends want to know what good is a man if "he can't take care of me, can't take care of his responsibilities, and can't take care of his family?" That means that even when she is capable of giving an assist, or the nature of the financial dynamics would make it more logical that she be the dominant contributor, it just "doesn't feel right." So, even in *our* self proclaimed independence, the contradiction in our experiences lies in the fact that we want to compete and act like men, but we still want to (and do) *feel* like women.

Chapter 4
The Social Contradiction

Women are from Venus, Men are From Mars, is a very telling statement and title. The planets that we find ourselves on are worlds a part because, as mentioned in the previous chapter, the way in which we are socialized is the polar opposite-from gender role socialization- to the lessons that we are taught. Hell, we can't even play with one another when we are growing up-gender segregation. When boys play with too many girls, he is labeled a sissy or gay. So in order to, in our own minds, deter his "sexual deviance" we deter him from playing with girls and begin to force traditionally "masculine" toys, games, activities and even behaviors on him-out of our own fears and perceptions that are completely grounded in the socialization process discussed in the previous chapter.

When girls play with too many boys she is labeled a tomboy or lesbian in earlier ages. And so, like the boys, parents and caretakers begin to deter the interaction out of fear. When boys and girls reach adolescence, if they are around one another too much they are either gay or promiscuous. For girls the interaction, like that in childhood is deterred because promiscuity either real or perceived is a breach of the cult of true womanhood-specifically the characteristics of piousness and purity. However, as long as the interaction expresses heterosexual tones, for adolescent boys it is less severe, or even acceptable and even celebrated as an identification of the male's masculinity. If the adolescent male is characterized as having feminine tendencies, the interaction is either deterred or ostracized. And then, as young adults we become distractions and threats to one another's goal fulfillment, i.e. graduating college without making or having babies, getting depressed or side tracked etc.

So the question is. How are we supposed to truly get to know each other's differences and socially constructed nuances before we get married, if we never truly socialize with one another until we begin to seek meaningful relationships with each other? And then how does that trial and error period that often ends in heartbreak three to twenty times before we find our husbands and wives effect our perceptions and trust for one another? And how does the damaged trust affect our ability to truly connect and embrace the concept of true commitment-not just the word- but the art and promise of commitment-especially "until death do us part."

The fact that girls are socialized to express and process emotions creates an issue because it is contradictory to the way in which boys are raised. A little boy falls down and busts his head open, he is bleeding profusely and you can see his skull and he starts to cry…we immediately tell him to "hush, stop crying *like a girl*. You'll be o.k.," encouraging him not to cry even in the severest pain. Even though this is an exaggeration, what is not is the fact that there has to be a visible ill or hurt for boys to be supported through their pain and allowed to actively express their emotions without criticism. He is supposed to be "tough" and crying and/or whining even when adults would is not being tough.

In essence, through that process, boys are being trained NOT to express their emotions. They are being trained to hold back their feelings and work through them internally, as opposed to externally-to process rationally instead of emotionally. Boys are being trained to believe the fallacy that emotion and expression are actions that are equated to femininity, and is hence taboo for them. They are being trained to identify the problem and fix it as quickly as possible with the least amount of toil. So consequently to their own selves as well as their relationships, they handle things completely differently than women- in the opposite manner. So not only do men and women fail to know one another, they fail to understand one another, and consequently fail to even be able to communicate and resolve conflict effectively.

On the converse, women are trained to express themselves, let the world know how they feel, and receive the support that they need while they go through it. Unlike the boy, a girl falls down and scrapes her knee. It doesn't even bleed, but she is crying profusely. The whole family rushes to her, encouraging her to let it out, reassuring her that it is going to be ok, kissing the "boo-boo" and treating it as if it were the gash that the little boy just got and needed 30 stitches for. She is kissed and when she is finished with her emotional and oftentimes overactive cry session, she is reassured and either protected from going back out to hurt herself again, or coddled as she re-enters the world. So, this is the way that she is trained and socialized to believe and expect the world to handle her pain. Consequently to the communication and conflict resolution process then, women fail to understand that it is not that men do not love or understand our plight, it is simply that men have a different way of perceiving, processing, and understanding pain and conflict, hence communicating through, and resolving conflict. It does not mean that they feel or understand any less than a woman.

Ladies, it is not that men don't want to hear us, it is that they don't want to hear us for a long time. We want men to *feel* our pain, and we want to *feel* that they feel it before we let it go. That's the way it has always been. And if we don't *feel* that, we will keep it going until we do. And if we don't, we leave the situation feeling empty or unfulfilled-believing that their inability to connect with us on "our own" level, means that they don't love or understand us. But, this is not true. It is that they are not trained to be the ones to nurture our emotions the way that our mothers and aunties and even fathers did. It is not their experience and so they can only do it the way that men do-that is to address the problem and resolve it as efficiently as possible.

He hurt your feelings because he did not hold the door for you when you went out to dinner with your friends. He walked ahead of you and did not hold your hand. You gave him the eye the whole time at dinner and pouted all the way on the drive home. When you got home you start the conversation by telling him about how he doesn't respect you and asking how could he embarrass you in front of Paul and Sheila. But, he doesn't know what you're talking about. "Yes you do, you know exactly what I'm talking about. You know exactly what you did." "No, I really don't. All I know is that you acted like a baby the whole night." "I acted like a baby!? Well what about you?" "I don't understand why you acted like that. Tell me what I did." "I shouldn't have to tell you." There is the breakdown.

Now instead of us saying that "I am angry that you didn't hold the door for me." We expect them to know what they did, and don't believe them when they say they don't. And then instead of telling them exactly what it is that they did, as they not only expect, but need in order to be able to process the issue rationally and effectively in their own minds, we give them the ambiguity that is a part of our often times emotional communication and conflict resolution style. This miscommunication is what most often than not turns the conversation and what could be a minor issue into one that escalates into an argument where the original problem gets lost.

Harvey asserts: "Men are not that smart." I disagree. Men are brilliant, just as women are. It's not that "men are not that smart." They are just simple creatures (and not in a negative sense either, so don't clap and agree). They just don't process as deeply, emotionally, and as erroneously as women do. As we are trying to figure out or interpret what they mean(t) by their actions and or what they say/said, they are doing and saying what they feel and think or doing something without feeling or thinking or processing the outcome as deeply as they should in order to avoid misunderstanding and miscommunication(which I have to argue is something that men should cultivate)-without any undertones or ulterior motives. So, most often, they truly do not understand or know, and/or truly disagree, with our assertions about their intentions. Why? Because, it is truly NOT what they meant.

We shut doors on people when we are mad instead of just saying we are mad. They say, we are mad-simply. Therefore, when they (men) shut or release the door on you (women), it was probably an oversight-the result of them not thinking-not an exemplification of any anger or intended disrespect.

The difference in the way in which we are socialized and conditioned to handle conflict, pain, problems as children directly impacts the way in which we communicate and manage conflict as adults. If men are socialized not to show emotion, if they are socialized not to deal with problems emotionally, if they are trained to be rational thinkers and problem solvers, how can we expect them to know how to be any different when they "deal" with women?

The nature of most, if not all, relationship and marital problems stem from this inherent conflict and contradiction in the manner in which we are socialized. And it is compounded by the fact that as the social, political, and economic conditions of society have changed, so have the requirements and gender role dynamics of men and women. Yet we are still being conditioned in the ways of old. This means that while socialization prepares men and women to take on the social roles of provider and nurturer respectively, now a days, it takes two incomes to run a family. Therefore, both must work and take on the roles of provider together-which leads to the next problem.

Consequently, in this shift, it is the woman who takes the brunt of the burden in this shift because- as studies and works, such as Hoschild's (1989) *Second Shift* suggests- even though most women must work in order to provide for herself and contribute to her family, men have not made the shift to assisting with domestic responsibilities and childrearing, which causes stress in the relationship.

To the cause of women, as a result of the continued traditional gender role socialization, many men believe that because they are men they are not supposed to adhere to and/or take on roles and tasks that are associated with femininity. However, just like a homemaker, when both must work, both must share in other responsibilities. And in today's era, most women, ***especially those who*** take on traditionally masculine gender roles, reject traditional "feminine" characteristics that are now deemed oppressive and demeaning, such as weak, submissive, domestic, and passive-and resist being controlled or dominated, even under the guise of being protected and provided for

More significantly, in cases where women have been raised in matriarchal families and have witnessed matriarchs carry the family alone for generations, those women do not feel as though they "need" a man at all. And so, accepting one as a partner

or husband comes with great expectations from men that are not always realistic, and

often times great adjustments to their own beliefs, cultural traditions, and values that are

rarely made. The result is a social contradiction that adversely impacts the nature and

depth of the relationship-which will be discussed in the next chapter.

Chapter 5
Acting Like A Man

Before I begin, I have to say that this chapter is specifically dedicated to my sistahs, and it's going to be a "keep it real" session that might get under some finger nails and make some uncomfortable. But the situation *has* to be analyzed from a cultural perspective, because it is a problem that is significantly affecting the African American community from social, economic, relational, and health perspectives. The problems include the divorce rate, the number of single parent households, the increasing rate of poverty that results from those single parent households, the increasing number of African American professionals who cannot find suitable mates and have not been married, the rate of infidelity in relationships and marriages, the inability or unwillingness to establish monogamous and committed relationships to the most pressing problem of the disproportionate and increasing rate of HIV infection in the urban community-specifically among African American women.

So, I don't mean to be exclusionary, but women of color have been almost completely excluded from professional research and literary discourse on relationship dynamics. The cultural dynamics of relationships have simply been absent from Dr. Phil, Oprah, Tyra, the View and other shows that delve into relationship dynamics and women's issues, and have been notably absent from the relationship and self-help literature-until Harvey wrote his book. And it is understandable because in many cases, I do not believe that many are really in touch with the influence of the historic racial and cultural dynamics that influence relationships in the African American community.

It is clear that there is a very real problem with what I will term *Black* love, *Black* connection, *Black* intimacy, *Black* relationships, *Black* monogamy, and especially marriage in the African American community. And it has become very apparent to me through the discussions-both formal and informal, that I have had with many African American women and from my own experiences- that women have created a new system of coping with the heartbreak and/or absence of dominant male figures that they have either witnessed, experienced, and/or wished and set out to avoid. And that coping mechanism involves "acting like a man."

I don't know how many times I have heard the statement "I don't need no man." As a matter of fact, I don't know how many times I have said it, even in raising my own son, as a single parent. And for Black women it seems to be an easy statement that comes with a conviction that is attached to the reality that-for Black women it is too common, and it is true. We have seen our mothers, grandmothers, and even, although to a lesser extent our great grandmothers raise children alone. We have witnessed them "hold the family DOWN" without even showing the stress and sacrifice that it took to simply "get by." We can all, and I mean all, bear witness to the strong Black mother because we have either experienced it personally or we know, some, if not many who have. And so, contrary to that traditional gender role, and traditional gender role socialization, we have been trained to always make sure that we can take care of self.

Now, while I believe that all women should be prepared to ensure that they do not have to be dependent on another, I must state clearly that this "training" has created a very counterproductive relationship dynamic in the Black community- because it is grounded in the perception that Black women cannot, and have not been able to depend on Black men, and therefore, must ensure that she is able to take care of herself and her family. It is further rooted in the belief that there has been a very consistent and prevalent absence of Black men in the home since slavery-which is COMPLEELY FALSE.

First, I must dispel the myth of the historical construct of the irresponsible Black man. I did the research for my dissertation and found that contrary to the infamous *Moynihan Report* (1965), Black men did not abandon their families as a result of the mental/psychological condition/ing of enslavement. As a matter of fact, after Emancipation and well into the 1950's, census data shows that African American men represented a significantly higher percentage of labor force participants than African American women (Spencer, 2005).

Figure 1

Black Women and Men in the Labor-force 1880 to 1990.

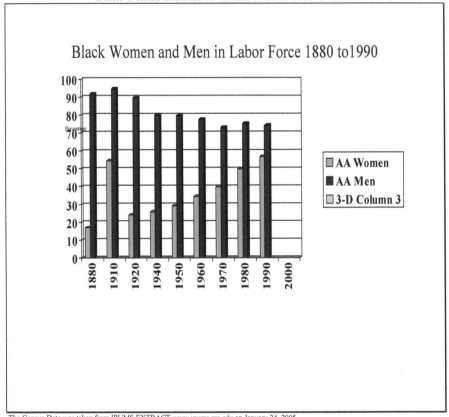

The Census Data was taken from IPUMS EXTRACT www.ipums.ms.edu on January 24, 2005.

Therefore, it is clear that the presumed inferiority, irresponsibility, and absence of Black men from the family was a fallacy, a stereotype, a social construct that was not a part of the African American experience.

I point this out for a very important reason, and that is to reiterate, and I cannot reiterate strongly enough that, contrary to what reports and pseudo research says about the historic condition of the African American family, enslavement did not destroy it. It merely forced African Americans to create new forms of family-extended family-adopted family-play family-matriarchal families, and even patriarchal kinships and brotherhoods. African American people were resilient. During the period of enslavement where there was forced separation of the family, forced breeding, forced removal of the children, forced gender segregation, forced denial of any union, African American people made a way to maintain family bonds and kinships. This forced separation was a necessary part of the institution of slavery, not an inherent part of the African American Experience. The institution of Slavery could not have existed and been successful if bonds were allowed to solidify, so for the ruling class elite, these institutional practices of separation and denial were necessary. And, African American people adapted, adjusted, and re-created new means of establishing bonds and kinships that kept the race alive.

The race did not become confused or brainwashed or dehumanized in thoughts and understanding. African American people did not selectively choose or become selectively brainwashed or conditioned to deny or reject family and kinship bonds. African American men did not use enslavement as an excuse to run from family and/or their rights and responsibilities as husbands and fathers. And African American women did not use enslavement as an excuse to deny the men that they loved and bonded with those rights. The Post emancipation movement/Civil/Equal/True Freedom Rights Movement for inclusion and equality contradicts the very essence of such an absurd, yet well accepted, assumption. Why would, or even how could, a race have the where-with-all to fight for freedom, equality, inclusion, social, political, and economic rights, and not be able to break the "mental bondage" enough to fight for family? How can one be brainwashed by the institution that they fought to dismantle.

However, when the institution of slavery was abolished, and African Americans were free to reconstruct their families, they did so without force, encouragement, or direction from any other. And in those families Black men fulfilled the social definition of manhood by being husbands and fathers, providers and protectors to their families. It was not until the transition from the Industrial through the Electronic to the High Tech era that the condition of the Black family began to change.

As the chart shows that, except for 1910 which was a decade that was marked by economic depression, Black men were predominant in the workforce and were thus caring for their families. The rates do not begin to balance out until the 1970's, which reflects the productive and economic shift out of the industrial era and economy through the electric era and into the high tech and global era. This shift resulted in a higher rate of unemployment as a result of the replacement and displacement of humans in the labor force. This coupled with the Social Welfare guidelines that forbade men from being present in the household in order to receive benefits is what led to the declining presence of Black men in the household. It is ironic that this type of welfare "rule" that contributed to the destruction of the Black family corresponded with COINTELPRO and other covert governmental operations that were designed to systematically deconstruct the urban community and the Black Power Movement.

And even though, I would strongly argue that way too many Black men are falling into the trap of embracing stereotypical constructions of Black manhood and Black masculinity that are destructive to love, relationships, and family in our community, I must reiterate that it is not a part of the historic root of the African American experience or the unparalleled legacy of African people.

So, now Black women (we) can stop hating. We can remove ourselves from the role of the poster children and spokespersons for the "Black Men Ain't Shit" campaign, so that we might move toward getting what we want out of our relationships and marriages, and rebuilding the family bonds, by being what "we" need to be, instead of acting like men in our various perceptions of manhood.

As I have stated throughout this book, I have conducted numerous informal focus groups, have had countless discussions in my courses, and endless conversations with my girls, and in them I have found a significant pattern that must be addressed. I have found that as a result of the pain that women have collectively suffered, we have started to attempt to engage in relationships with men, like men. Follow me.

Many of the themes of the conversation center around the disappointment in/with men, and how we are going to begin to use men just like "they use us" so that we what? Make sure we don't get hurt. In essence, the rationale behind this shift is that we assume that if we "play the game" this way, when the relationship ends, we are going to come out with as much of ourselves in tact as possible. The argument is that women can use men just like men use women. And the sad thing about it is that way too many women believe this can be effectively done. But can it really be done without consequences?

The previous chapters were ordered in that way for a very important reason. From the chapter on the four states of being to social contradiction, each illustrates the components of self, and the way we are socialized for the purpose of illustrating how the social constructions of gender shape our characteristics, desires, and identification of how we view and define our selves as women. I wanted to specifically highlight the "social contribution/influence" of how we identify our femininity, why we desire to find a suitable partner, and how we strive for marriage (and hope for a fulfilling one, but will settle), and family as the critical pieces of defining and/or completing us as women. How marriage and children become the completion of our womanhood, no matter how much we've accomplished in our lives, is embedded in our social experience.

Now, I know many women will stop here and begin to think. *"I don't need no man, I don't need no man to complete me. Hell, I don't even know if I want to get married. All I need is a little nookie every now and then and then he can go the hell home."* We can talk about self love and independence all day; but the reality is that many women do not *feel* complete until they are married with children, whether they *act* like they are cool with it or not. We may be o.k. with self without a relationship, but we desire them.

Women's perception and conversation about Oprah Winfrey is a prime example of this. Even when we don't want to acknowledge or admit it in our own lives, we can analyze the predominant discourse about other women as an example of the validity of this assertion. Oprah is one of the most successful women in the world. She is well established as an entrepreneur, philanthropist, and in her career as the leading talk show host-globally. However, when women are sipping tea and the claws are out, the discussion about Oprah turns to her personal life-specifically her relationship. The fact that she and Stedman have not gotten married, and the fact that Oprah does not have children stands at the forefront of defining her femininity. Most assume, and would argue, that she "sacrificed" those things for her career-which would presume that those were things that she desired but was not willing or able to achieve in conjunction with building her "empire." It is difficult for many women to fathom that perhaps she does not want to get married, and maybe she did not want children. It goes straight to "Stedman doesn't want to marry her, and/or it's too late to have children now." It has even gone so far as women claiming she is "selfish" for not having or adopting children, and/or that questioning her sexuality. How many tabloid articles, internet posts, and conversations have circulated those notions?

Although many value her "material and career" success, even women do not value her "femininity" and "womanhood" because she is not married and doesn't have a family; and therefore, does not represent those socially defined characteristics of womanhood. And those concepts and identifications of womanhood and femininity are socially constructed ones that we all attach and/or relate to on one level or another. They are so engrained in our society and socialization process that it is virtually impossible to completely escape the influence.

So, we have to be real -with ourselves-about how we are truly defining who we are and what we want. Think about it, we've all heard or even said it before "I don't need no man, I'm my own woman." But that's the problem because the same women who will assert or agree with that statement are the same women who will be the first to vehemently barge in on the *"All men are dogs, Black men ain't shit"* conversation.

The reality of it is this! If, and that is a strong if, the ability to act like men was a real part of our being, if women were *really and truly* able to adapt to this type of interaction, we would never have the "men ain't shit" conversation. We wouldn't be bashing Oprah's or any other woman's decisions about marriage and family (because I am sure that there is no shortage of men who would love to marry Oprah). We wouldn't

be lining up to buy Steve Harvey's or any other book that defines the problems with

relationships or analyzes or talks about what/how men think. We wouldn't be at the self

help seminars on building healthy relationships and improving self or the religious

retreats asking God to find us a partner. We wouldn't be watching Oprah, or Tyra, or Dr.

Phil, and we wouldn't not be at the chick flicks, shaking our heads, smacking our lips,

and mumbling at the male antagonists in movies like Waiting to Exhale, Not Easily

Broken, and every 50 million dollar-in the first week- grossing Tyler Perry movie ever

made. We wouldn't because we would not be able to relate to the characters' experiences

because we either never had the experiences, did not know anyone who had, and/or had

the experiences but did not care- and so we would not have any emotion or connection to

that type of content. The fact that we seek these types of books, seminars, retreats,

movies speaks to the fact that we can relate-simply. And we can relate because every

woman has either directly or indirectly experienced the things that are portrayed and

discussed in those forums in one way or another.

So, before we can help ourselves, we first have to be honest with ourselves. We

have to admit and then tell the truth. We can relate to all of those things because we are

MAD AS HELL! Go'on, admit it. We are mad at relationships, we are mad at love, and

we are mad at men. Yes! Scream it!!!!! I AM MAD AS HELL! We are mad at every

man, including our fathers, who abandoned us, walked out on us or our mamas, let us

down, stood us up, breached trust, lied, cheated, stole, abused, betrayed, broke our hearts,

and/or murdered our spirits. And we are mad because we didn't think we signed up to be

abandoned, walked out on, let down, stood up, breached, lied to, cheated on, stole from, abused-emotionally, psychologically, sexually, or physically, betrayed, crushed. We did

not sign up to be murdered- to have our ability to love (our hearts, spirits, and souls)

rolled under the wheels of an 18 wheeler on the highway or a jumbo jet at take off!

So, instead of trying to figure out "self" and how we contribute to our own

disappointments, we become victims, and get together and support each other in our own

victimization by making it ok to point the finger at men and rationalize our shit, instead

of understanding the fact that no one can do to you what you don't allow. So, in response

to the history of collective heartbreak, we have come up with the "bright idea" that we

can avoid the pain of relationships and love by putting up the wall and/or to trying to

change how we play the game. Now I am sure that all are shaking their heads in

agreement and feeling it. But, it gets deeper.

We believe that changing the way we play the game means that we now remove

most of our "selves" from love, connection, commitment, and approach relationships

from a physical perspective. So we take our hearts out of the equation, put it in the safe

and lock the safe in the attic. And then we use our minds to manipulate the situation and

interaction of the dating game. But most importantly, we _completely omit_ the presence,

much less the guidance of any *Higher Power* as we navigate the rough and murky waters

of relationships and intimacy. Dangerous. So what do we expect to come from that type

of interaction?

We believe that changing the game is to "deal" with men the way that we believe

men "deal" with us- to not only as Harvey's title suggests "think like a man" but act like

a dude. We believe that we can be "friends with benefits, that we can detach ourselves

from any emotion, emotional/mental/spiritual desire, all the while convincing ourselves

71

that we do not want commitment and/or marriage (but we will get pregnant and have his baby though). And many of us have either tried, or are still playing this game. What do we *expect* will come from this? We have to expect nothing because that's what we are putting into it when we engage in this way-nothing. If we engage physically, we can only expect the physical- remember, we will reap what we sow

This is the depth of it. If that's what we really wanted…If that's the way we could adapt to acting…If we could really act like (our perception of) men. If all we truly wanted was nothing, why in the hell are we still mad??? This is so simple, it almost gets too deep. When something does NOT bother you, it simply does not bother you. A person does not get emotional or develop feelings when the action or attitude or interaction of/with another does not affect/effect that person-period. The emotion grows from the internal discord that an individual feels when something doesn't set well within her. We feel when something touches us. It touches us when it matters. What do I mean? Let me give you a common example.

You meet a guy at the club (or library or church for the club naysayers). You exchange numbers. He is beautiful, intelligent, successful-and most of all attractive "to you" in all of your ways. Imagine it…..But, he's too good to be true, so before you even engage, you determine that you are not going to get close. You are going to play him before, or even while, he plays you. The two of you talk on the phone and you ask him if he's seeing anyone. He tells you that he is dating but he doesn't "have a girl." (Now right there if you are clear and honest with yourself about your own expectations, this is crossroads number one.) But, because you have already decided that you are going to play your cards tight to the vest, you have taken your heart out locked it in the safe and hid it in the attic, you are using your brain to (what you believe will be) manipulate him, and have blocked any Higher Power from guiding or intervening. Because you have not been honest or real with yourself about your own expectations, you start to see him "casually" anyway.

After a couple of conversations the two of you start to hang out. If you value sex with you as a bargaining chip, you will either dole it out or withhold it as you see fit. So, on the third, fifth, or twentieth hang out, you invite him over. (Now right there if you are clear and honest with yourself about your own expectations, this is crossroads number two). On the day that he is expected to come over, you have "the discussion" with your girls…and like ya' girls (who are just as lost and confused as you) will do, they support the following dumb ass decision… "Girl, I'ma put *it* on him (translation: I'ma fuck his brains out). I went and got my little Victorias Secret set, lighting the candles, and playing the (insert your favorite mood music here) CD." And you convince yourself that this move is all about your "physical needs." (Now right there if you are clear and honest with yourself about your own expectations, this is crossroads number three.) So, he comes over and you all break the sexual ice.

Now breaking the sexual ice is an extremely important transition because it introduces the expectation that sex and/or intimacy- in any of its forms- is going to be/become a part of the "friendship." It begins the shift from friends to friends with benefits, which usually poses a problem for many reasons. But, let me continue with my little scenario.

So, the two of you embark on this "relationship," and it's all good while you are getting the attention that you need and desire. But, it always brings up a crossroad where not thinking things through or keeping it real causes a fatal collision. If you tire of him first, then things work out fine. If he starts feeling you and expresses his desire to have a monogamous relationship with you and that is what you want, things work our fine. But, if those outcomes do not occur, the crossroad meets at the intersection of your "relationship" (and I put that word in quotes for a reason) being challenged by his other female friends, girlfriend, fiancée, or even his wife-or you wanting to define/redefine the relationship so that you become or even begin to work toward becoming his girlfriend, fiancée, or wife, and not getting the response that you want. What do I mean? Let me give you a harsh, but real example.

He was just at your house on Thursday night, the dating had subsided before you invited him over. So, you invited him over for a reason- to use your sexual charm to re-ignite the relationships. But, even after that the dating still diminished and the two of you became no more than sex partners. But like women do, you have convinced yourself that all you need is a little nookie every now and then and then he can go home. So, you are using him "just as much as" he is using you. So, you have sex and when it is over that's what he does-go home. (Oh don't say it couldn't be you, think about it. You can relate.)

You don't tell your girls, but you have tried to reinstate the dating on numerous occasions, but he is always too busy etc. You have even tried to deny the booty calls, but you just can't because denying the booty calls means that you don't get to see him at all. So, you convince yourself that you just need him for sex, when in reality you would rather have that piece of him than nothing at all. So, Friday night after he tells you he's hanging out tonight and can't get with you, you decide to go out with your girls. You go to the club and see him all hugged up on/with this fly woman, who looks just as good as you, or hell, not as good as you. BOOYAH!!!!!!! Wipe the sweat off ya' neck.

This scene reminds me of the scene in *Two Can Play That Game*. Now, this is the reality check-the point where the contradiction between what women feel, and how women act have a head on collision. This is where the truth comes out. And see we all forget the truth when it comes to the collision. We can all finish the story here. The first thing that happens is your girls look at you like what you gonna do? And everyone gets angry at whom? HIM. The woman instantly becomes the victim, he becomes the perpetrator, and the other woman becomes the conspirator who is at the helm of him "doing this to you."

We have to remember though, you had already decided that you were going to play the game like a man. He neither lied nor deceived you. He told you from the beginning that he was dating and he never took it back or expressed a commitment to you. You still made the decision to not only see him anyway but to take it to the next level by giving him your most precious gift for absolutely NOTHING. But, you had that under control... all you needed was a little nookie every now and then. You weren't feeling him and you weren't expecting anything from him, not a commitment or a relationship-right? So why is there a collision at that point, or any other point that resembles that point? Even if you were at his house having sex with him and another woman knocked at the door or came in the room. There was not an implied or expressed commitment. There was no contract or warranty. It was an "as is" "day to day" connection. So, in reality, there should be no conflict.

If all of these assertions were true, and everyone understood the implications of playing the game that way, there would be no feeling from you *or* your girls. You and your girls would be able to look over, the same way a dude would look over at a "jump off" that he was "hitting" and truly cared nothing about, and not care who she was with. But, most women would not be able to do that, so the situation would not "go that way." The issue would be, "he was just at my house last night having sex with me, and tonight he's with that B?!. Oh is he doing her too?. Awww…hell naw." The question is <u>why</u>? <u>Why</u> does it matter?

The second really harsh example is this. After several months of engaging in this "friends with benefits relationship," you decide you want to have "the conversation." As Harvey states, you hit him with the dreaded four words "we…need…to…talk." In justifying this "change of heart" you decide that there is too much going on in the world, and you want to be his only one, or you state that you have developed feelings over the course of time-even though the reality of it is that you wanted to be with him (in a monogamous relationship) the entire time. You were just "playing the game." So, in the morning, you ask him how he feels about you. He tells you you're cool and he enjoys hanging out with you (except you all don't really hang *out* that much, more like hang *in*). When you ask him about solidifying a committed relationship, he informs you, in a detached tone, that he is not looking for a relationship, and reconfirms and reminds you, for his own ego's sake, that he told you that in the beginning. You instantly get enraged because you have given yourself to him. (You said that it was just nookie, when in reality you were using your body to convince him that you are the one). So, you start to question him and he tells you that he is seeing other people, sleeping with them too. And you can't believe it. After all of these months he's been sleeping with you and other women too. He's been taking your goods and he doesn't even want to commit. So you curse him out and kick him out of your house and call your girls. And everybody gets mad at who? HIM! The woman instantly becomes the victim. But again the question is why. The answer: because it matters. The question is why does it matter?

Just like harsh example one, you set the tone. No matter how you try to justify it, *you* set the tone by trying to act like a man. This is the break down. If women could really "act like men," if we were able to truly "play the game" like a man, we would not be mad. Simply. The reality of it is that we are tired of being hurt and disappointed. We say we are tired of being disappointed by love. But, we are, or at the least, we should be tired of being disappointed by our own selves, by the continuous counterproductive decisions that we make in our interaction and relationships. We are tired of being disappointed. But again, it's our fault. Let's break down these harsh, yet very real examples.

We make conscious decisions from start to finish on how we will go about interacting in our relationships or relationship building. The problem is that because of our hurt and our negative perceptions of Black men, we have constructed a way of dealing with Black men that is just off. We try to convince ourselves that by "acting like they do" we can either protect ourselves from heartbreak by protecting or detaching ourselves from connection, gaining as many tangible things from the relationship as possible so we feel "up" when it's over, or soothing our egos while we use our bodies to "buy the time" to establish a connection that we hope will grow from the physical to the spiritual and/or simply convince him that we are "the one." But men said it, they will very rarely wife a "jump-off." So, how does our playing into the role of a jump off, in our efforts to act like men, work toward our goal. Answer: It doesn't.

As mentioned there were several situations where a woman who finds herself in that situation, can make vital decisions. But, those vital decisions can only be effectively made *if* the woman keeps it real with her "self" about her expectations, goals, and the objectives of the relationship. The problem is that most women are not honest with self.

Crossroad number one: If you truly do not care about or want a man, you would not be looking, searching, surfing, waiting, praying, or crying over or for one. You would not be devising schemes to play the game. You wouldn't be spending all of that money on your hair or outfit so you can go to the club, or Weekend-Essence, All Star, Jump Off, so that you can be attractive to---men. You would simply not engage. So you must ask yourself, why are you in the game, if you truly do not want to play? What is your real/true motivation?

If your motivation is to find a partner that you can build a relationship that may lead to marriage and family with, then walking into it trying to fool yourself into believing that that is not what you want will be counterproductive. First, you will emit energy into your actions and interactions that will basically either say that "you're cool with whatever" or some ambiguous energy that does not allow the man to know where you are coming from. If you are clear about what you want then, you will be more diligent and vigilant about what the man says. In essence, if you are honest with yourself, you can be honest about the nature of the interaction. Therefore, you will be able to receive that when he says he's dating and/or not interested in a relationship for whatever reason...he means it. And so, if you are not interested in casual dating, you will understand that you must move on. You will embrace the fact, not possibility, then that if you continue the relationship you are taking a gamble on a chance where the odds are drastically stacked against you. So, crossroad one, if the woman was true to self, she would have simply said, "nice meeting you" and walked away.

Crossroads numbers two and three: Women can try to play the physical game if they want to, but there is something about the nature of allowing a man into our being that evokes/invokes the inner spirit. Whether we embrace our bodies externally or not, there is something sacred and emotional about sex for women. Perhaps it is the very nature of what it entails (which will be discussed in a later chapter). But, women have learned to use their bodies, to use sex to manipulate, negotiate interaction, believing that it is "the way." Let women tell it, women have been trained not to give it away for free, so even when we are not receiving material or money from it, we are using it for something. The question is for what---to procreate, to express a deep connection and love, to sustain our marriage, to satisfy our need to feel intimacy, to get the man to like us??? Women have to understand that as good as punani is, it never makes a relationship, and is the most faulty foundation that a relationship can be built upon. It's like the house made of straw, it can be blown away or burned down with one light wind or spark. It is engaging at the lowest level, using the lowest state of being, which means that it will yield the lowest outcome or return.

In true love, sex (or better- making love) is an expression of that love, it is a supplement to otherwise fulfilling relationships, in a casual relationship that has no foundation, it is just a means to get one's rocks off, a minimal and momentary experience that has no meaning. So, if the woman's purpose for deciding to have sex with a man is to find love and commitment, we have to be honest about it. It is only then that we will realize that sex *never* makes a relationship. And if we really understand this reality, then we don't give away something that we'll want , but can never get back if it doesn't end the way we envisioned, either consciously or unconsciously.

Professional women have a unique set of issues as well that stem from the assertion that one should choose a like partner. They are often caught in the crossfire of embracing middle class values and being confined by the historic disenfranchisement of the race. So, as women achieve status, the pool of eligible and compatible men decreases-especially in the African American community. The assumption that women embrace then is that if you get an advanced degree or start to earn double figures, you better already be married.

As a single professional (educated) woman, I am consistently asked how I feel about the problem that professional (educated) Black women face in finding partners. The question is based on several very prevalent stereotypes and issues. (1) There are more Black men in jail than college. (2) Most Black men are on the down low. And, (3) the professional and "well-to-do" Black men prefer women of other racial and ethnic groups. So, consequently to the professional women, the question truly being asked is how do professional Black women find suitable partners? All of these statements are fallacies that serve to create a fear and distrust of Black men and hence interfere with our willingness to connect.

However, the greater issue is professional women's perception of what a good partner will be- a perception that is also based on the manner in which we are socialized. Because women are socialized to first embrace the male role of provider, not just Black women, but professional women in general face the dilemma of finding a man who is "on her level." The inference is that a woman is supposed to "marry up"-that is to find a partner who has achieved the same or greater status than she financially and/or academically. Where the issue poses a greater problem for women of color has to do with the percentage of African American men who pursue advanced/graduate degrees, reach higher levels in the corporate and professional world, and the income differential/disparity between Black men and men of other races. But, the issue again also lies with the way that professional women view themselves and how they define their expectations.

It is true that pursuing intellectual and professional growth often delays a woman's ability to focus on marriage and family. It is ironic but contrary to Harvey's assertions, I argue that women, not men who are driven by the ambition to achieve professionally and academically, are the ones who may put off marriage and childbearing until she has achieved her desired status. I argue this because women must make the physical and social sacrifices to accommodate her family that men do not. For example, pregnancy and nurturing infants, especially for women who breast feed, requires that women take time off from what they are doing to give birth and nurture, especially in the first few weeks of a baby's birth. Socially, it is expected that women will, as has been discussed in previous chapters, be responsible for sacrificing self for family, and will put work and professional development off to ensure that her "family comes first."

It is also argued that in the pursuit of her professional, academic, and/or intellectual goals, professional women become more set in her ways, more competitive, more detached from traditional gender role characteristics, and perhaps even increases her expectations about what she wants in/from a man and in a relationship. Therefore, when she enters the "dating game," she establishes and follows a different set of rules that can also be counterproductive to establishing beautiful and healthy relationships and marriages. Some of the most predominant ways that these counterproductive traits manifest is through the Control Freak, Hood Saver, and Queen in Waiting personas.

(Control Issues): Either a woman will assert such a strong sense of independence and control over her own life and space, that although she invites men into it, she does not create the space for the man and the relationship to peacefully co-exist with her independence and control.

(Hood Saver): In such she will not bond well with a man who takes on the traditional construct of manhood and masculinity because she will view his protection and provision as a threat to her control over her own life and space. She will even go so far as to convince herself that his attempts to, simply, "allow her to be the lady" is his attempt to demean and/or break her. So, she will divert to someone that she can control through her "taking care" of him. She will seek a man of, what she perceives to be, "lesser" value because he may not have achieved the social, educational, or financial status that she has; but he will have other attributes that will make him acceptable to her social network- he will have the infamous "potential." In this type of relationship, instead of accepting him for who he is, she will look at him like the empty foreclosure. She will evaluate his "potential" and her definition of that potential will be based on her ideal of what a man should be. So she will try to mold him into what she wants him to be, change him- often times in a demeaning or condescending sense. She will maintain control by continuing to reinforce her belief that she doesn't need him, she can put him

82

out at any point, while simultaneously developing a sense of resentment and disrespect for his inability to be a man-a sentiment that is most often expressed in arguments where she verbally emasculates him. Consequently, she will not be able to establish a real connection, hence a healthy relationship or marriage with him.

(Queen in Waiting): Or to the contrary, a woman will seek a man who she perceives to be just as good, if not better, than her. If she has a Masters and makes 80,000.00 a year. She will look for a Doctor or a Lawyer who makes 230,000.00. If she has a Ph.D. and makes 100,000.00 a year, she will look for a Ph.D., Doctor, or Lawyer, or Entrepreneur who makes 500,000.00 a year. His status will be of the utmost importance and the principle measure by/through which she will determine whether he is even "datable." This type of professional would not be caught dead with someone "beneath" her because that would her look like she is settling. In such, she would rather stay or pursue an unfulfilling relationship with this "type" of man than to understand that the foundation of a relationship must be based on more than his status.

(This aspect can also be attributed to women who may not have financial currency but have beauty that they use as currency.)

There are many Black women who "get their own shit," accomplish great things and are financially secure. However, the problem is that some act like their accomplishments define who they are, or they believe that they do. They can't even have a conversation with a brother without telling them about what they do, the house they have, the car they drive, the degrees they have and on and on. The message is I don't need a man, with the precursor being "a man has to have something to be with me." And then the conversation quickly shifts to "what do you do?"

Now, it is not that this is not an understandable, or even a necessary, question. As stated in the previous chapter, all women have been socialized to, or at the least, have an understanding of the social constructs of gender. The concepts of woman as nurturer and man as provider, is a fairly universal gender role construction. Therefore, just like other women, African American women also desire a man who will take on his role as a provider and protector. However, for African American women the term "gold digger," comes to the forefront when they embrace and desire those social expectations.

So, before I move on, I must dispel the misinterpretation of the "gold digger" construct because I think that it is most often applied out of context. A "gold digger" is a woman who wishes to use her assets to find a man to, not only provide for her, but to provide luxuries and a material and lavish lifestyle that she would not otherwise be able to or wish to achieve on her own accord. It is a term that was developed to define the women (or groupies) who spend much time seeking rich, high profile men with social or street status. However, over time the term has evolved into a label that is applied to any woman who expects something/anything from her man.

She wants her date to take her to a nice restaurant then she is a "gold digger." She expects a gift for Valentines Day or her birthday then she is a "gold digger." She expects a man to simply carry his weight in the household then she is a "gold digger." She expects her child's father to pay a reasonable amount for child support, she is a "gold digger." In essence, this term has become a convenient scapegoat for men who either do not wish to contribute anything materially to the relationship, or wish to condition their women to accept and expect mediocrity or irresponsibility as the standard. Consequently, by embracing the misuse of the term "gold digger," African American women are counter-conditioned to avoid, rather than accept and encourage men to take on the social role of a manhood and masculinity, by making them feel guilty for wanting, asking, and/or even accepting material or financial gifts or basic support and contribution from a man.

This is especially significant for professional women who, like other women, have been socialized to desire a provider- but have the contradictions that come with being independent and having to negotiate what it is they truly desire from a man, and what they truly want in/from a relationship. The establishment of professional status and independence sometimes creates an internal conflict about how professional women will define their own femininity, what their roles will be in a relationship and/or marriage, and specifically, what level of perceived "control" and "independence" they are going to be willing to "release" in order to develop a mutually respectful and reciprocal relationship, marriage, and family that does not deter her from her career.

The question becomes does being "a professional" mean that women cannot be "ladies" if that is what they desire. Or does it mean that being a professional means that they cannot truly love or be loved by a man who may not be at the same status level, but one who brings other contributions that would make a beautiful and mutually rewarding and fulfilling relationship? If a woman pays more of the bills because she earns more, does that have to mean that she is being used? Does that mean that a man is "less than" a man? Does accepting traditional gender role values mean that a woman cannot/should not contribute more to household expenses, even when it would be simple to do so? Or does it mean that she should act like a man, simply because she is able to, or has achieved a status that is more central to social identifications of masculinity.

On a physical level, women are not men. We are not socialized to be, or act, like men. Our temples are not constructed to be used as tools because they are connected to our emotional and our spiritual selves-even when our spiritual is not developed. That means that we can try to store our hearts in the attic, and engage as if it ceases to be a part of our being if we choose to, but ultimately it could and most often does prove detrimental. That means that our canals and wombs cannot be used as currency in this market/social exchange without consequences and conflict because it is attached to something greater within us.

On an emotional level, sex alone does not provide the emotional connection or intimacy that we either consciously or even subconsciously crave. It is really the closeness- the kissing, hugging, petting, staring, touching, the connection that sex brings that makes it meaningful. On a mental level, we are socially constructed to desire the interaction and institutions of marriage and family that define us as women. Therefore, much of what we do is based on increasing our "marriagability" through exposing us to potential partners and making ourselves more marketable. Consequently to not only the social perception of women, but our perception of self, the stigma attached to our detachment from our feminine values and constructs, does not allow us to be and remain comfortable with the permanence of acting like men. It is only acceptable as a means to an end. Which leads to the real question, what is the end?

The "end" is the goal and it is exactly why it matters. It matters because from the beginning we know exactly what we want-and it is NEVER nothing. Dating is the exploratory part of finding a good partner. Relationships are the road that leads to the goal. The goal for most women is to establish, through a relationship, a deep and

86

meaningful connection and experience with that person, to experience and build a relationship that will ultimately lead to love, marriage, and family. And that road is supposed to be exciting and rewarding. It is supposed to be an exploration that uncovers truths and treasures and even obstacles that allow us to learn more about not only others, but our own selves. That is the happily ever after, to see if he is "the one" that we want to spend the rest of lives loving and being loved by- the man that we truly want to be our partners, husbands, best friends, and present and loving fathers to our children. It is not supposed to be an exploration of a series of dead end relationships that crack and break our hearts with each end-until we have no more.

And that is why we are mad. We are mad because too many of our relationships don't end up the way that they should. Why. Because "WE" want and pursue relationships with those who do not have any intention of committing to us, who cannot/will not/do not/are not able to reach that happily ever after with us. We subsequently and consequently have children with those who have no connection to us as women-much less any connection to us as mothers to their children- which then transfers to their connectedness to their children because having a baby does not change the way that he feels about us, or his original intention. It only breeds further resentment for and toward us for actually forcing him to be accountable for his own failure to think with his brain instead of his penis. And we even marry those who never loved us or gave us anything more than their physical presence…And we expect it to turn out fine?

Well we have found that it doesn't turn out fine. It never does. Relationships that are based on superficial ideals, values, interaction, do not turn into fulfilling, loving, mutually respectful and rewarding relationships. The anger comes from the fact that even though women attempt to "act like men," when we "feel like women." So the "act" is counterproductive to our own true goals and desires.

In acting like men when we truly desire to be treated like women, we contribute to our own discontent and disappointment. That is what I needed Harvey to say. In denying what we truly want in our hearts, by pretending that we don't need or want or desire loving relationships, we contribute to our own discontent and disappointment. That is what I needed Harvey to say. We can't excuse ourselves or allow others to excuse us from our own contribution to our problems by shifting the focus completely away from our own shit. We contribute to the dysfunction in our interaction by allowing those fallacies to not only shape our own identifications of our self and worth, and the nature of our relationships, but to influence the destructive decisions and patterns that we make and develop in the "dating game." The reality is that if you feel like a woman, you cannot be or stay true to acting like a man. My gay brothers will re-confirm that.

Chapter 6
If You Want A Butterfly...You Have To Be
. . . .

Didn't India Arie paint such a beautiful and necessary picture about the dynamics of energy and karma in her song *Butterfly*? To most, her lyrics are just a song...But to analyze, to really hear her, is to see the light that illuminates the path to beautiful.

How much clearer does it need to get? This is the story of reciprocal energy and interaction. You will get what you give, reap what you sow, so you have to be conscious of what you are "planting" because the seed you plant will be what you grow. Too many people are not conscious of who they really are, what they really want, and what type of energy they exude for whatever reason. Even when people are just "cruddy," they justify and rationalize it, but feel victim(ized) when the reciprocal energy continues to manifest a negative existence for them-a negative life. That is why truly understanding and embracing the four states of being is important. That is why Arie and Harrington's lyrics are so profound.

When one becomes conscious of the four states of being and analyzes his/her own presence based on that, he/she will be able to define the areas/states that need to be developed and utilized more. Specifically when one hones in on that spiritual being, and understands that there is something that operates within the universe that is greater than our own self interest, that person will evolve into a higher state of being that will allow them to truly transform their lives and the lives of others. This will then ensure that the quality of that individual's relationships and life will be truly enhanced.

89

There is a reason why only five percent of the world's population reaches the state of actualization or the spiritual state. This is because most do not embrace the importance of actualizing or developing their higher states of being, much less focus on developing her own character. It is commonplace for most to point fingers and blame others for our situations and experiences. Therefore, most do not reflect on how our own decisions influence those experiences. So, we never actually realize the power of our own decision making on the quality and control of our experiences.

Growing, interpersonally and spiritually, is reflected in the metaphor of the butterfly-specifically the metamorphosis that caterpillars go through to become the butterfly. If a caterpillar survives long enough by slinking along on the ground (existing at the lowest level), he will find the tree immerse himself in a cocoon and emerge a beautiful butterfly-free to fly (exist, live the rest of her life) at the highest level. It is in the cocoon that the caterpillar goes through his transformation. How beautiful is that?

While the metaphor is beautiful, it reflects a very intricate process-the process of recreating the self, shedding the old skin and developing or growing another that allows elevation and flight. The reality is that if we are to truly make transformations in our own lives and beings, we must often do so in a safe and uninterrupted place and space. We cannot evolve while we are still intricately immersed in the chaos of our former existence. Let me say that again, if we are to truly make *transformations* in our own lives and beings, we must often do so in a safe and *uninterrupted* space. We cannot evolve while we are still intricately immersed in the chaos of our former existence.

What that means is that we cannot try to find ourselves and transform ourselves in the confines of dysfunctional, distractive, and counterproductive relationships. We cannot remain with those who have been enabling our counterproductive ways and decisions. We have to be free to first do our own homework, define our own selves and expectations, and then do the work of transforming our energy, hence -who we are.

We have to go inside of ourselves first and do intra-reflection- that is looking inside ourselves to analyze our strengths and weaknesses- the things that are productive and counterproductive to how we are relating and living. We then have to fix it by developing our higher states of being-mental and spiritual, shedding the negative characteristics and embracing the positive so that *that* energy precedes us.

Most importantly to the nature of our relationships and the development of self, we have to simply-'be real" with our selves about our expectations of relationships, men, love, intimacy, sex, self perception, and the intricate question of how we "use" our bodies-as women. As mentioned in the previous chapter, we cannot exude the energy or promote the perception that we do not desire the things that we do desire. We cannot be physical and not expect others to only or predominantly relate to us on the physical. If we do, we cannot become angry at the reciprocal consequence. We cannot secretly desire love, and get angry when it does not bloom from the deceptive seed of "sex" or physicality. We cannot secretly desire a relationship, and get angry when it does not bloom from the deceptive seed of friendship. We cannot secretly desire to make intimate love, and get angry when it is not produced from plutonic superficial sex.

If we want love, we have to express and expect love. If we want commitment, we have to be clear in our expression, engagement, and pursuit of commitment. If we want husbands, we have to prepare to be wives. If we want to make love, we cannot "fuck" before we even know his last name, or use our bodies to try to invoke love or worse, gain

91

materially. In essence, we cannot begin a relationship by stating that we want to be friends, invoke benefits, and expect love and connection to grow from that. It almost never happens- and I would not bank on the almost and believe that you will or even can be the exception to the rule.

Further, we cannot change our story in the middle of an already established "friends with bene's" relationship and expect our "friends" (men) to change with us simply because we gave the benefits. We cannot use sex as a hostage or barter without first establishing its worth through making it an expression of our priceless being. More importantly, we cannot "fall in" love during this process and expect love to love us back. Deception, either self deception or the deception of others, is simply not the fertile ground from which love can or will grow. It was not the seed that we planted, it was not nourished by pure intention, and so it will not grow or will never be healthy.

So, if we want a butterfly, we have to be a… butterfly because nothing falls out of the sky. That is we have to be what we want, be the energy that we wish to generate. We cannot play games with ourselves, others, or love. We simply have to keep it real. This is the first and most important-simple step to achieving the quality relationship and love that we desire.

Chapter 7
Embracing Your Queendom and Protecting Your Temple

The Mantra

Ladies, place your hands over your wombs and repeat after me.

I am a Queen and my womb is my Temple. Call me Isis for I am the Goddess of Life and Fertility. I am the Earth. It is through me that The Most High has given me the most blessed ability to bring forth the most precious gift of- life. So, Life is Gods gift not my own. Therefore, my canal is "a most precious path" and my womb is the most sacred temple. It is through my sisters (of all races, ethnicities, and religions) that this world, that humanity, continues to be. If my presence ceases to exist, then so will all "man" kind, for no "man" can be born without me. So, I will never minimize my SELF and what I mean to this Universe-nor will I allow any man to minimize me. I will embrace my Queendom and protect my temple, and he who is blessed enough to enter will have no choice but to do the same.

When one thinks about sex and intimacy within the existing context that society has placed it in, it is easy to become sidetracked, distracted, and derailed. Lust has replaced love, infidelity has replaced faithfulness, multiple partners has replaced monogamy, dating has replaced marriage, single parenthood has become the new definition of family, and mothers have become the new dads. But, there is no wonder why love, intimacy, connection, commitment have become the ideal as opposed to the real, the exception rather than the rule, the sub-culture rather than the cultural norm. Society has placed sex and women's bodies on a strictly physical level. The media has completely objectified, sexualized, and commodified the woman's body-especially the hypersexual displays of Black women's buttocks, in urban media.

This has created a dynamic where these images have been, and are being, internalized as an identification of women "taking agency" (taking control) over their bodies and sexuality-being free. Women have mistakenly embraced these images as a means or identification of "self expression" and/or self control- not understanding that the reality of it is that we have lost control and allowed the men who dominant the media to shape how we are identified. The truth of the matter is that those women who are in the media are being used to sell a product- be it a movie, a CD, a car, or shampoo. They truly have no control over the presentation of their image at all. And those who are embracing the media images are being misled into allowing those in the real world to treat her as an object as opposed to the subjective being that she is.

Somehow, the "so called" feminist and sexual revolution has been misinterpreted, and the misinterpretation has given rise to the misperception that it meant that women should no longer value their bodies and subjectivity and rather "use" it as a means of achieving an end-no matter what the end is- from reaching an orgasm to "landing" a husband. By shedding the notions of the cult of true womanhood- somehow the revolution symbolized that piousness and purity was something to be rejected. And in such, we have truly diminished the value of our own bodies, sexuality, and ultimately sacrificed our own divine purpose and even our own emotional needs.

Given the social construction of "a woman's worth" there is no wonder why people would just as soon have sex before they even know the persons last name, much less know who that person really is. There is no wonder why sex has become a mandatory part of "getting to know" another, "dating," and/or even "friendship. It is as if everything in society says *that* is the way, and then compounds the message by making it easier to engage in activities and relationships that are counterproductive to the concepts of love, commitment, marriage, and family.

The internet- by way of internet porn and dating sites- makes it easy to establish superficial relationships that amount to nothing-temporary hook ups. It has literally become the modern day pimp. The utilization of sex, "sexiness," women's bodies as objects, commodities, and advertisements for every product from shampoo to auto parts, has really desensitized us to what valuing our bodies and "having sex" really means. The introduction of birth control methods have allowed us to divert, minimize, and even negate the most predominant purpose for sex-procreation. We have become a nation of people who have really and literally created an existence where we believe that physical stimulation is the predominant and most important reason for having sex-to the extent where we believe that- like an addictive drug-we cannot do without it. Consequently, we have truly become desensitized to understanding what really transpires during these very delicate and sensitive moments. But most importantly, as women, we have forgotten what our bodies really are and what it all really means- that is on a spiritual level.

This mantra is not designed to be some spiritual mambo jambo. But, it is designed to allow us to understand what- a precious gift- we have, hence what a precious gift we are. It is not about how we can use what we have, or who we are. It is about embracing the gift and understanding that the gift is so much higher than the physical and emotional tool that we use it for. So, let's break down the mantra.

My mother sisters will be able to understand the significance of placing your hand on your womb. There is nothing more powerful than to literally watch a baby develop and grow inside of us. NOTHING compares! There is nothing more powerful and sacred than to place your hand over your womb when the baby is inside so that you can feel the baby move. Even when the baby is not moving, we place our hands on our wombs to pass our energy to him/her, to speak to him/her without words. Touching our womb is enough to remind us of what a blessed gift we have inside of us…what a powerful responsibility we have to protect that gift…and what a sacred and fragile place our wombs are at that time. At the moment we realize that we are nurturing life, we "innerstand."

But, it is the same womb that we've always had. It is the same womb that we had when we were born. The womb did not change when we conceived. It did not miraculously become that sacred place *after* we conceived. It was sacred all along. The place where we cradled, are cradling, or will one day cradle our babies and nourish them to life, is the same womb that we've had all the time. So the question is? How have you cared for and nourished the womb that your baby will one day gain life in???
Ahhh….will he/she be cradled in a sacred place, or will he/she be cradled in a tainted place, a place that harbors negative energy and experience? Will he/she be cradled in a

place that has been nourished by love or confusion, peace or chaos? As crazy as this may sound, think about this. If your womb could speak, what story would it tell, what energy would it provide?

The significance of placing your hand on your womb (and even encouraging your partner to do the same-before engaging in sex) is to remind us of its divine purpose and significance. It takes the canal out of its (physical) sexual context and puts it in its spiritual context.

I am a Queen and my womb is my Temple.

As women, we have to begin to redefine our own selves in a manner where we first feel and embrace the power of our being as women, our own womanhood. We have been minimized for too long, and we must understand that treating ourselves and/or allowing others to treat us like objects or whores does not make us powerful. I am a Queen, one who deserves respect, reverence, adulation, honor-yet protection, love, and support. As a Queen, I deserve, and have the right, to be recognized as being somebody-a multi-faceted and multi-dimensional subject and not a homogenous, solely sexual, object who is on this earth to simply satisfy the sexual or physical needs and whims of others. As a Queen, I take my place "beside" a King, which also has great merit. If I embrace my Queen, then I will not just choose any one to sit beside. I will only sit next to a King.

There are several basic definitions of "temple" that I'd like to borrow from Dictionary.com- (1) Any place or object in which God dwells and (2) something regarded as having within it a divine presence. But even outside of the more formal definitions, a temple is a sacred place, a place that is dedicated to a Higher Power, a place of worship

97

and a place to be worshipped simply because of the power of the presence within it. It is the last place that we would ever enter recklessly, nor would we allow any other person to enter a temple in our care recklessly. It is not a place wherein we would litter, spit, disrespect, or much less defile.

When we think about what our wombs really are, when we think about our biological makeup as women-think about the anatomical or biological characteristics that make us women, we put our wombs back in context. Our womb and canal are integral parts of our reproductive system. Again, together, they are the nurturer and passage way to life-simple but deep. The womb is the place where we nourish life until our children take that journey through the canal (unless we've had a C-Section-like I did) to reach *this* world-taking their first breath-where the umbilical cord-that direct connection- is cut, allowing them to begin their journey toward individuality.

Within that womb, we are helpless in the development of our babies. While we can take care of our bodies, making sure to eat properly, exercise properly, rest, not injure ourselves, see the doctor, not stress and on and on, we really have no control and no insight of what is going on within our wombs as our babies grow. What goes on inside of the womb is truly divine. No matter how much we may respect our obstetricians and the power of the sonogram, the stethoscope, the fetal monitor…what happens in the womb is divine and guided by something completely outside of our own selves. Creation or procreation is the most powerful example of the existence of the spirit. Therefore, as dictionary.com states, like a temple- the womb "is the place in which God dwells, it is a place that has within it a divine presence." The womb is a temple. So should we not treat it as such, even when we are not "with child?"

If we understand and embrace this reality, how can we justify using our priceless wombs as tools to manipulate unworthy men. How can we allow much less welcome strangers to enter, deposit, and defile our temple? How can we allow the media and society to define and establish how we must govern and protect our "selves," our temples?

> *Call me Isis for I am the Goddess of Life and Fertility. I am the Earth. It is through me that The Most High has given me the most blessed ability to bring forth the most precious gift of- life.*

While many argue that Isis was a mythical figure, Isis was a Queen, wife to Osiris, deified the Goddess of Life and Fertility. The ankh- from which the current symbol of "female" is derived ♀- the symbol of life and fertility is linked directly to Isis. It was a symbol that she is constantly pictured wearing on the walls pyramids in the hieroglyphics. Like the earth, the place where seeds are planted and nourished and then bring forth life, Isis represents that same process. So, like powerful Isis, like the beautiful and powerful Earth, a woman is the human vessel by/through which God has given the human race the gift to nurture and bring forth life. So like a Goddess, like the Earth that allows humanity to exist in the Universe, the presence of a woman is divine because her "blessed" ability to bring for the gift of life- is divine.

> *So, Life is Gods gift not my own.*

When we "innerstand" how precious the gift of life is, when we "innerstand" how precious our purpose is, we will "innerstand" how precious and divine our bodies are. Life is God's gift. The ability to bring forth life is God's gift. Therefore, our body's are God's gift, not our own. We are just the managers or hosts if you will. So, will we manage, treat, and protect our bodies like God's gift, so that we can host our children's spirits in a pure, clean, and peace environment? Or will we abuse it, and allow others to abuse it? When we begin to value the gift, we will not allow our "selves" to be minimized by anything or anyone. When we truly recognize and embrace how beautiful and powerful our purpose is to this Universe, we will become "sickened" by how our images, our bodies are distorted, objectified, minimized as some sexual commodity that is just present for the visual and sexual pleasure of others. How can our buttocks' which is only significant for emitting waste and our breasts, the tools that we have been given to nourish our young become the principle identifiers of our womanhood? Where we will expose them, enhance them, exalt them? How can we allow those that we give birth to-men-to defile our presence?

Therefore, my canal is "a most precious path" and my womb is <u>the</u> most sacred temple. It is through my sisters (of all races, ethnicities, and religions) that this world, that humanity, continues to be.

More importantly, when we re-frame what our bodies and our sexuality really mean, we will view intimacy as a gift- a gift that is priceless. And just like any priceless gift, we would not just give it to anyone. If our canals were a precious diamond ring that was passed on from our great grandmother, we would never give it away. But, diamonds are not priceless. Our canals are the pathway to life in both directions- so intimacy and entering that precious path is priceless. If we embrace that then we must be mindful of what energy we allow to invade that "most precious path." If our wombs are the most sacred temples, our earth, then we have to be mindful of which seeds we allow to be sown in, or even pass through, that womb. We simply have to take the power and control of our bodies and images back.

If my presence ceases to exist, then so will all "man" kind, for no "man" can be born without me. So, I will never minimize my SELF and what I mean to this Universe-nor will I allow any man to minimize me. I will embrace my Queendom and protect my temple, and he who is blessed enough to enter will have no choice but to do the same.

Once we embrace our own power, we must then take the lead in re focusing others' perception of us. Not that I want to go into any type of feminist rant here, but please let's not get the game twisted or allow others to twist the game by trying to minimize who we are or make us feel guilty when we claim it. Without "womankind," there is no "man" kind. No man can be born without a woman. No man can bring forth life. So no man can or should be left to define who we are as woman. No man should be allowed to destroy our being because we have failed to uphold our being. The truth of the matter is that when we take the lead, first as individual women and then as a collective, in re-establishing or re-creating our essence, others will have not choice but follow.

Let me elaborate. Many women now feel that they must succumb to this sexualized dating scene or be alone. Many women have argued that they conform to the sexualized standards of dress, the sexualized standards of interacting so that they will be able to "find" and/or keep a man. If they don't wear the skimpy clothes, he will be attracted to someone who does. If they don't have sex or "do tricks," he will find someone who does. So, even when these acts and values may be contradictions to a woman's own internal value system, she conforms anyway out of fear that not conforming may impede her ability to find a partner. And in such, she loses a part of who she is. She diminishes her own self worth both externally and internally for what? If a man is one who will seek superficial then he is superficial, so why diminish one' self for nothing?

As was discussed in Chapter 1, this is most often not the case. Men question promiscuity when it comes to defining or differentiating what will be a sexual relationship versus what will be a meaningful one. Subsequently, as discussed in Chapter 5, if we hold misperceptions about what men think, then we conform to value systems that do not achieve our desired goal of finding husbands and establishing beautiful and healthy families and perpetuate and validate men's own perceptions that they can engage physically with us without consequence.

We cannot be afraid to be alone for a while. We cannot be afraid to admit that our sexual interaction is not about simply reaching an orgasm. It is not just about "the physical" because even studies show that most women do not reach orgasm every single time and that an orgasm itself can be more easily achieved through masturbation. We first have to acknowledge that it is through intercourse that we seek intimacy, closeness, and that sacred bond that happens when a man enters our most sacred place. The goal is not the intercourse, the goal is the connection. We are looking to "make" and or express and feel-love. But, we will not achieve love or lasting connection through intercourse. So if the connection is a strictly physical one, it will end as soon as the connection-intercourse- is done. In such, we will be forced to seek intercourse in order to allow that connection to be continuous. That is where promiscuity becomes an issue. We will not find or secure love through using or allowing our bodies to be used. At best, we will experience a momentary high that will lead to a harsher crash, if we are not clear and have not separated the difference between having sex and making love (which will be discussed later).

But most importantly we have to embrace our Queendom and protect our temple. If we do, we will automatically represent and present that energy which will, in turn, guide our interactions. It will define who we are and define our expectations. Ultimately, by valuing our own divine presence as women, by valuing our sexuality and intimacy, by placing our temples at the highest esteem and protecting our temples, others will have no choice but to do the same. I said if we all set the tone, others WILL HAVE NO CHOICE, but to do the same.

Chapter 8
Planting Your Most Precious Seed or Throwing Out Your Trash

Now we must divert attention away from the woman and focus on men. I could not allow you (men) to escape without any culpability. One of the most common things that I have observed as a Sociologist is the absence of men's understanding and awareness of how they perpetuate dysfunction in relationships, and an almost complete absence of taking any real responsibility for how they abuse their own bodies. It is as if this notion of the hyper-sexuality, promiscuity, and/or infidelity of men is natural, biological or innate. Even Harvey promotes the notion that "men are just sexual by nature." And it seems as though the world believes it. There is something attached to the Y chromosome that makes it natural for men to act like animals when it comes to sex.

Yet in discussions that men have, they are quick to assign negative characteristics to women who are viewed as promiscuous. They find and sincerely express morals and values when judging women. But, hypocritically fail to use those same morals and values to govern and guide their own behavior(s). *She* is a whore, hoe, slut, smut, jump off, skeez and on and on. But you (men) do the same, and you are not???

Why? How does that really work? How can men selectively find and utilize morals and values. Either men have them or not. Animals do not. They do not have the capacity to utilize human logic, assign morals and values to actions and behaviors. They are not able to process what humans consider right and wrong. There are no labels attached to cats who have litters by different cats every time they are in heat. It's the

104

animalistic nature of not sex, but reproduction. For animals sex is driven completely by the biological and/or physical nature of animals need to procreate. This is done by emitting pheromones in the air or water to create an environment where they can reproduce, hence keep their species alive. This is so because they do not have the ability to establish and negotiate relationships and interaction in a humanistic way. But human beings do. That, again, is what separates humans from lower animals.

The contradiction or the assignment of the innate nature of "the dog in me(n)" is nothing more than a fallacy created to excuse men from their conscious decisions to engage in relationships in an animalistic manner. So, the contradiction must be pointed out and accountability must be established.

The greatest contradiction is the way in which men are socialized to so readily assign negative labels to women who are open sexually or even promiscuous. As mentioned above, in discussions, focus groups, and debates, men are quick to call a woman a whore, hoe, slut, smut, or whatever new term emerges. But, it is somehow alright, o.k., and even cool for a man to have sex with a woman that they have labeled as such, or believe has a questionable sexual value system, without consequence to his own character.

The argument is he is just being a man. And in the discussion, he will be valued, while still "bashing" the "whore" that he has had sex with. No one questions how he must perceive or value himself to enter someone who he views as being impure because in stating that he is just being a man, and loose sexual values are natural for men, he is excused from his own humanity, his own manhood. It is just like the principles of reasoning states if A=B and B=C then A=C. If men are loose sexually. And being loose sexually is animalistic. Then men are animalistic. But, men are not animals because being animalistic is not subjective. It does not rationally turn on and turn off in different situations. Animal and human are mutually exclusive terms and beings, they cannot co-exist. You cannot be both at the same time or turn one off and one on when the situation suits. Men are rational, logical beings with the capacity for thought. So, being animalistic or treating himself animalistically is a choice that reflects a flaw in a man's character and in his decision making process. That is because he makes a conscious choice to operate on the lowest state of being. Ahhh, you see how those chapters start to fit together. Don't get mad and close the book gentlemen.

Let me speak to my soldiers for a moment. What does it say about you when you are willing- and make a conscious decision- to enter a woman that you do not respect, a woman who you have determined has allowed her womb to be invaded and contaminated by so many others. More specifically what does it say about you when you have assigned such a negative value to a woman and yet that is where you plant your seed? And then you get mad when she comes up pregnant and you cry as if *she* tried to trap *you*? The whore becomes the mother of your child.

Think about it, what does it say about you? It says that your need to stimulate yourself superseded your judgment in such a way that you made a conscious decision to put your "self" and your seed in the womb of a whore. DAMN! It is a sign of the ultimate weakness, that is the weakness of spirit, mind and the weakness of body. And it is not cool, or o.k., or a sign of your manhood or masculinity to be able to "count bodies" because in counting the bodies of the women, you are defiling your own. Let me say that again, in counting the bodies of the women, you are defiling your own.

Let me "keep it really, really real" for just one second. Would you dip your chrome rims in acid every time you washed your car? I will trust that your answer would be absolutely not. Why? I will trust that your answer would be because you value your rims and you paid a lot of money for them. So, why wouldn't you dip them in acid? I will trust that your answer would be because the acid will destroy the rims more and more each time you dip them. You know where I'm going. So let's put it in a sexual context.

Do you value your dick? Do you truly value your seed, sperm—the life that each of the millions that you emit each time you ejaculate represent. What is a whore? She is someone who has been entered and discarded in many times. So, one could make the analogy that her canal and womb are acid. If a woman's womb became more acidic with each encounter, and you could visibly see your dick losing its shine or coat or width or length, or even worse if your dick would literally burn like dipping it in acid each time you entered and impure and unclean canal/womb, would you act like an animal then? Ohhh-ohhh, I know the answer. HELL NAW!!!!!!!! You would become really rational and discriminating about the way in which you use your dick. It would probably force men to re-direct their whole way of embracing their sexuality and masculinity. But, because men cannot actually see the damage that they do to their own selves engaging like animals, it is more comfortable and easy to simply rationalize the behavior by embracing such absurdly demeaning characteristics…"I can't be faithful, I'm a man." "We are just like that, it's a part of being a man." "I'm a dog by nature." "There's just too much pussy to commit to one." "I wish I could fuck every girl in the world."

So, since it is clear that you are not an animal, let's spiritualize who you are as a man.

The Mantra

For the purpose of this mantra, the key represents a man's penis. I chose the term "key" because a key is essential to entry. It both locks and unlocks, without resistance, what is protected. And it is assumed that once it is locked none without a key can enter. That was too deep, read it again ladies and gentlemen. In this case the penis represents a part of the body that is designed to enter the womb to unlock not just the pleasure, but most importantly, the gift of life in a woman. It is assumed that when a woman gives a man the gift of entering her body, she has given him the key to her canal and womb. More significantly, when she decides to allow a man to plant his seed in her womb, she has given him the key to unlock her ability to create life within her. POWER! A key to entry is either made because what must be entered belongs to the individual who holds the key, or has been given to the individual who holds the key. If this entry occurs within the beauty of a monogamous and committed relationship or marriage, when he leaves her, his key will then lock the door and no one else can enter. Her canal and womb are protected by him. Conversely a key only works for one door, unless others have identical locks. But no house, or car, or safe, or locker will have the same key. Therefore, the key that is designed specifically for entry in one womb does not and cannot work in another. So why even stick it in the hole? FIYA! But, y'all don't feel me though. The key is the most essential and valuable part of belonging and protection.

So...Men put your hand on your temple. Oh, don't get iffy now! You do it at the basketball court, when you're walking down the street (like you have to make sure it's

108

still there), when you are looking at a sexy woman, when you're rapping, when you're on the couch while you're watching the game, and when you're sleeping so... Put your hand on your temple and repeat this mantra.

I Am A King, A Warrior, A Father, A Protector. <u>That</u> is My legacy. My Key is my Temple. It defines my male, but it can never, alone, define me as a Man. My Key is the blessed vessel by and through which The Most High has given me the most blessed ability to give my Queen Life; but, it is my strength to carry out My legacy that makes me a man. So, I am life and life lives in me. Through my key, the book of life in my Queen is opened. Therefore, my key is a most precious path and my seed is divine. Through the most sacred connection, I remain divinely connected to and responsible for the most precious temple that I enter and the most blessed life that I create. For the gift of the Temple and the gift of life are God's gifts, they are not my own. So like a Soldier, I must protect my key to her Temple, the Temple, My Queen, and my most precious seed. I will not take My Legacy lightly. I Am A King, A Warrior, A Father, A Protector. That is my legacy.

I Am A King, A Warrior, A Father, A Protector. <u>That</u> is My legacy.

African American men and women have specifically been hoodwinked about the legacy and history of our ancestors/ African people. Due to the need for slavery, (and that is providing a source of labor to produce agricultural resources for British and French Industry), as mentioned in the last chapter, the legacy of African people had to be deconstructed and destroyed in order to promote the agenda of European expansion, colonialism, and capitalist development. This was necessary in order to support the notion of European and White supremacy that has served as the foundation for the enslavement and oppression of removed African people, and the colonization of the African continent-under the Berlin Treaty (1884). The stereotypes of biological inferiority and the savage and animalistic nature of African people was necessary to remove those who needed to be the agricultural producers in the United States, Central and South America, and Caribbean from their subjectivity as humans because it was against God, a sin, to enslave a human.

The truth is the evolution of the human race has its origins in Africa. Not just the ape or the Australopithecus; but the homo-erectus and the homo-sapien. The oldest most organized and developed civilizations and the ability to produce existed in Africa long before Asia and Europe had a populous of humans. Religion (monotheism), Science, Mathematics, Astrology, Astronomy, Medicine from pharmacology to obstetrics and gynecology, Language, and Agriculture are all a part of the legacy of African people. Not that the point needs to be belabored, but many do not know. People of African descent com from a legacy of Kings, Warriors, Priests, Farmers, and Commoners, and Slaves just like Europeans do. We come from a legacy of largely patriarchal societies where men provided for and protected the women, not in an oppressive way but in way that allowed women to be "queens" "mothers" and "wives." So these historic experiences are not just unique to the European. So all people must embrace the true legacy of the all people, not just the reconstructed racist ideologies that served very distinct productive and politico-economic purposes. If the powers that be will not disseminate the truth through our mainstream political, educational, and social systems, educators must do so- so that the legacy of a "race" of people can be resurrected and we can stop grounding our perceptions in a reconstructed history of a people that was created to justify the institution of slavery, colonialism, imperialism, and expansion, and continues to be the ignorant foundation of racism and prejudice today.

My Key is my Temple. It defines my male, but it can never, alone, define me as a Man.

Just as a woman's womb is a temple, so is a man's penis-his "key." It is not just some detached rod or stick that's designed to test the depth or temperature of some water he cannot see into. At its lowest level, a penis- not a key-is an integral part of a man's physical and biological being. It is connected to his biological construction and so any damage or injury to it will cause pain to "the man" it is attached to. Therefore, unlike a detached tool, it is safe to assume that one would measure the risk of using "body parts" as such. With that, it is feasible to question, if a man would not dip his penis in acid, or even chance dipping his penis into a substance that he was unsure of-one that could potentially harm him, why wouldn't he exercise that same discrimination his sexual relationships with women?

Y'all didn't hear me though, so let me repeat that.... With **that**, it is feasible to question, if a man would not dip his penis in acid, or even chance dipping his penis into a substance that he was unsure of-one that could potentially harm him, why wouldn't he exercise that same discrimination his sexual relationships with women?

Like grandma says, "all that feels good isn't good for you." Although men may not be able to see and/or even feel the damage that is done by using his key or his temple as a penis, a rod or a stick- to test the waters of every woman that moves his physical, it also defiles him as a man, and all of his being. Real Talk: It's not just about predisposing himself to a host of diseases and infections that may show up when he urinates, or in swabs or blood work or not. It's not just about using the condom to protect himself from the physical risks, the same as an individual would wear oven gloves so he doesn't burn his hand in the stove. It is about understanding how the loose sexual practices and habits of a man are NO different than a woman.

Although it is historic and somewhat universal, I argue that in today's era the promotion of men being defined by their sexual conquests has become far too prevalent- across racial, ethnic, class, and cultural lines. It is as if a man's penis has become his sole identification of his manhood. While it is the predominant identification of his male, it, alone cannot define him as a man. To be sexual and have no other value as a man or even a human does not make a man. To have many children and have no connection to them does not make a man. Even socially, a man is defined by his ability to take on certain social and economic roles in the family, community, and in society. A male (which can be animal or human) who has children and does not take care of them is not valued as a man. A male who has sex and has no other value to the environment is not valued as a man. If you think your penis defines you, you are just a male, you are no MAN.

My Key is the blessed vessel by and through which The Most High has given me the most blessed ability to give my Queen Life; but, it is my strength to carry out My legacy that makes me a man. So, I am life and life lives in me. Through my key, the book of life in my Queen is opened. Therefore, my key is a most precious path and my seed is divine.

This is probably the most significant and deep part of the mantra because it is the part that calls and speaks to the spirituality and consciousness of men. Men have to stop objectifying their "key." As mentioned above, it is not an object, it is not a tool. It is a blessed vessel. It is the part of a man's being and anatomy that is the most important to the survival of the human race because it is the vessel that carries the seeds of life-something that is also minimized. And even though we create these short and superficial terms for a man's sperm-cum, giz, whiz, cream (or whatever), and even though there are way too many encounters where men spill it haphazardly-through masturbation, in condoms, on backs and thighs or other places of senseless and meaningless sexual encounters, and/or even in the wombs of women they have defined as whores-a man's seed is living and it is life-abundantly. A man's seed is divine.

A man's "seed" are soldiers that have the capacity to seek an egg. They are actually living organisms that compete with one another in the womb to create life. It brings the life to the dormant egg- a union that brings life. Think about it, we are all the results of this union. So a man's seed is not spit, or mucous, feces, urine---it is not, nor is it comprised of bacteria or waste. Why treat it as such? If the key is the temple, then the seed that the temple holds, protects, and transports is divine. When it is being thrown away, discarded, wasted- a man is throwing away, discarding, and wasting life. He is throwing away, discarding, and wasting the divine. When it is placed in its spiritual context, it ceases to make sense, right?

Through the most sacred connection, I remain divinely connected to and responsible for the most precious temple that I enter and the most blessed life that I create.

When sex, is spiritualized and put in the context in which it is divinely intended, when it is viewed for what it actually is and what actually occurs during sex, it becomes more than just a physical stimulation or a pleasurable sensation. The union between a man and woman, the connection that "making love" not just sex- represents the most sacred connection. And a man must be responsible not only for his own key, but he must be responsible for taking care of the temple that he enters, which means taking care of his Queen. Most importantly, he must be responsible and divinely connected to the life that he creates. But this depends on the nature of the union.

One cannot spiritualize anything that comes from a strictly physical connection- not the womb or the children that may be conceived. If a womb is entered in anger, hate, or detachment, how can one find attachment to not just the act, but a child that is born from that anger, hate, or detachment? Even at its basic, sex is for procreation. At its highest, making love is a divine connection between two people who share the deepest bond. A man who loves his wife and witnesses the divine blessing of life created by the two of them, will love that life because that life is a physical and biological manifestation of the two people united. But, that's too deep for many.

If men STOP objectifying sex, conception/procreation, and the lives that are created (children) and begin to embrace sex as the divine and blessed connections and lives that are created, the family can be reconstructed. If this is done, men will also begin to be discriminate about the women that they chose to connect with. If they had to be connected to their children they would be more discriminating about the wombs in which

they plant their seed because in under that frame of thought it would be asinine to plant

his seed in a woman who would not be a beautiful and committed mother to his child.

For the gift of the Temple and the gift of life are God's gifts, they are not my

own. So like a Soldier, I must protect my key to her Temple, the Temple, My Queen,

and my most precious seed. I will not take My Legacy lightly. I Am a King, a Warrior,

a Father, a Protector. That is my legacy.

As was discussed in the chapter on the 4 states of being, when people begin to

understand that there is a higher being to which we must be accountable, that the things

that we so often take for granted are divine blessings-when we people begin to put things

and experiences back in their original and divine as opposed to these social and sexual

contexts, we will have no choice but to begin to reshape the way that we live and

experience the gift of life and existence on this Earth. I know this sounds so "Baduish,"

but we really have to understand what these things really mean.

The body as a whole is the most divine organism, and then the body's ability to

create life through the union of men and women, male and female is also divine. The gift

of our lives or our ability to create the lives of others is not our own gift, it is God's gift.

And we cannot claim to be God or even Godlike when we are not even close to living the

will and purpose of our Higher Power, of our Creator. So we cannot claim to be

responsible for the gift.

Is the purpose or the definition of a man, making babies that are left without

fathers, without his presence, guidance, nurturance, protection, love, respect, adoration, commitment, engagement? How many children across racial and class lines are psychologically, physically, and spiritually abandoned by the men who created them? How are boys supposed to learn to become men, learn what it means to be a good husband and a good father without an appropriate and stable example of that in the home? How are girls supposed to learn what the nature of healthy relationships and marriages are supposed to be about, what they really look and feel like? How are they supposed to gain an example of the healthy love of a man? How many girls and women are still searching for their fathers in every man that continues to shape how they perceive men, love, intimacy, commitment, and marriage? How many women are really seeking the love, acceptance, and protection that they never received from their fathers-which become you- through their sexual encounters with you? How do you as a man reinforce the disappointment of women? Do you men simply blame women? Do you not see the significance of your role as a man?

When did it become o.k. to leave women as the sole nurturers and providers for the children? What universal law or rule allowed men to be absent simply because they do not like, get along with, are not with the women that they consciously planted their seed in, whether they intended to create life or not? What universal law made it "an option" for men to be fathers if they felt like it, or if the circumstances were amenable simply because they do not have the capability to carry, give birth, and breast feed their own children? These practices are simply taking the human race back to the animal kingdom-this is creating an animal kingdom among human beings.

That is the way male animals act naturally, they impregnate without commitment and connection to the mothers of their children or their children because their mental state does not allow them to do otherwise. So the question becomes are you a male or a man? If you embrace the divinity of your role and capacity, you are a man. If you continue to live using your penis and cum as waste, or to create lives that you abandon, you are a male.

Men must step up and embrace their legacy and responsibility as MEN! A man will use his key to express love and protect his Queen. He will STAND to love and protect the life that The Most High- the original Creator- gave him the capacity to create. That is his divine purpose. That is his responsibility to not only his Queen but to the Most High. How about if God came down and said to all men, I command you be responsible for any life that you create, would that change the way in which men use and/or abuse their temples and discard their seeds both without and after conception.

The last part of the Mantra backwards reads:

I Am A King, A Warrior, A Father, A Protector. That is my legacy. So like a Soldier, I must protect my key to her Temple, the Temple, My Queen, and my most precious seed. I will not take My Legacy lightly. For the gift of the Temple and the gift of life are God's gifts, they are not my own.

POWER!

Chapter 9
What is Love?

I am sure that you all thought I forgot. As mentioned in the Introduction to this work, I stated that this song was born out of a collision between my course and reading Harvey's book. As I stated, I toyed with allowing my students to define and discuss their definition of love, or whether I wanted to do something different. At 3:30 in the morning, the definition that I will introduce came to me.

I had been having problems because I could not find, nor could I construct a definition of love that encompassed, at least, what *I believe* love entails. And, I cannot profess to be the expert, because this definition and this work is about my professional and personal opinions, experience, and beliefs. And I could not find a definition of love in the literature or the dictionary that I believed would encourage people to begin to add the depth and meaning to the "term" that brings it to life and makes us accountable to and for it.

Even much of the literature and works on relationships agree that defining and/or conceptualizing "love" is one of the most difficult tasks. Many even avoid attempting to define it, even when discussing it and relationships. But, how can we discuss, and more importantly experience and engage in something that we do not understand? And how do shallow definitions positively or negatively contribute to how we perceive, engage in, and conceptualize love?

Here are some of the most common definitions that I found. In Dictionary.com, the first three definitions are:

1. a profoundly tender, passionate affection for another person.
2. a feeling of warm personal attachment or deep affection, as for a parent, child, or friend.
3. sexual passion or desire.

The key term in the first two definitions is "affection." This term is problematic for me because affection is something that must be expressed physically. And most often, people have very clear definitions or expectations of how "affection" is expressed. To me, it is the physical manifestation of love, it is the expression of love; but it does not define what love is. Attachment is also something that is the result of love. Significantly if one loves, he will be attached to that person. But again, to me, it does not define what love is. Definition three is extremely problematic, and is the focus of this book, sexual passion and desire, is strictly physical, to me it neither defines nor exemplifies love, but can be a manifestation of love. It is extremely problematic because if one embraces that definition of love, he/she will define love in a strictly sexual way and justify sex as the predominant means of giving and or receiving love. But, as mentioned earlier in this work, sex never sustains or builds love or relationships. Therefore it is important that the two remain separate entities, or at least the hierarchy that separates the spiritual nature of real love from the physical nature of sex be explicitly defined and expressed.

These definitions, for me, do not grasp the deep and spiritual nature of love. The definition of love is defined by Wikipedia in the following manner:

"**Love** is any of a number of emotions and experiences related to a sense of strong affection and attachment. The word *love* can refer to a variety of different feelings, states, and attitudes, ranging from generic pleasure ("I loved that meal") to intense interpersonal attraction ("I love my boyfriend"). This diversity of uses and meanings, combined with the complexity of the feelings involved, makes love unusually difficult to consistently define, even compared to other emotional states.

As an abstract concept, *love* usually refers to a deep, ineffable feeling of tenderly caring for another person. Even this limited conception of love, however, encompasses a wealth of different feelings, from the passionate desire and intimacy of romantic love to the nonsexual emotional closeness of familial and platonic love to the profound oneness or devotion of religious love. Love in its various forms acts as a major facilitator of interpersonal relationships and, owing to its central psychological importance, is one of the most common themes in the creative arts."

While this definition is more comprehensive than that in dictionary.com, it still uses the terms affection and attachment. It further relegates love to the lower states of being, the physical and the emotional, also attaching terms such as pleasure, which generally entails satisfying one's physical desires, needs, and/or cravings-be it through a meal, drugs, or sex. The definition does, however, support the difficulty of defining love, and although limited includes the notion of religion, and acknowledges the existence of a platonic love. But again, this type of love is taken out of the relational context and placed in a context that relates to a familial love or a reverence and love for the religion and/or religious figure in an individual's life.

This leads to the problems that I continue to have with the definition, it is as if those attempting to define love refuse to look at love from a perspective where all of the components of love, or all components of the ways in which love can be expressed can co-exist or be balanced. In these definitions, erotic love must be physical, but a non sexual love must be the type of love that is reserved for family. This type of definition leads to the assumption that an erotic love must include sex, and a platonic love must not. But in the context of intimate relationships where real love is present, those who express it state that their husbands, wives, partners are their best friends. They can sit next to one another and not say a word for hours but they can feel each other. They connect

120

mentally, spiritually, emotionally, and then physically the union is beautiful. So definitions that attempt to compartmentalize the types of love and make them mutually exclusive do not work for me.

So in my quest to develop a definition, I guess while I was sleeping, I wanted to create a definition that incorporated what love could actually be if we embraced what it is. And this is what I came up with.

Love is a deeply rooted spiritual, mental, and emotional connection to another. It has no boundaries and is not limited or guided by time. It is a connection that appears ethereal as its origin is divine. In a relationship its presence and growth can be grounded in the mutuality and reciprocity of the connection to and interaction with another. As an action, love is the art of expressing the (deeply rooted spiritual, mental, and emotional) connection- in ways that can be measurably received by the other-be it physical, intimate, material, verbal or otherwise. "In Love," love always guides and supersedes the physical, emotional, and the mental connection; therefore, true love/real love could never be superficial, untrustworthy, dishonest, deceitful, or painful. It exists independent of, and is therefore not influenced by, any other factor.

Many ask if I believe in love at first sight, in soul mates, if I believe that one can just know at that moment that he/she is the one. I do. However, the problem comes in when people do not have grounded perceptions of love, and/or handles and balance in/with their four states of being. This imbalance is what most often leads to the confusion and or disappointment with those who confuse love with infatuation, lust, or physical attraction- which are all strong "emotiono-physical" responses to something or someone that is pleasurable.

121

But, love is not a feeling of lust that occurs when you see that person who just fits your physical ideal of a mate. It is not driven by sexual desire or physical attraction. So my question for those who believe that they have experienced any of those phenomena is what makes you think that you are in love? What do you love about that person? What was it that you felt at that moment? Define the experience. These questions are usually telling about where a person truly is and how he/she is defining what Raheem DeVaughn calls "the love experience." They are also the questions that usually reveal that the individuals perception of "love at first sight" that "soul mate" or that "knowing was just an emotional response to some visual or physical attraction, it was not love.

I am also asked, "does love have to be reciprocal to be love?" My answer is absolutely and unfortunately not. One person can love, or be in love, with someone who does not and is not in love with them. That is another problem. Love is nurtured and grows in reciprocal relationships. But unfortunately loving someone does not ensure its reciprocity and it doesn't make a relationship work. People think that just because "you" love someone, the relationship is supposed to *be*. Well as we all should know, we cannot make people love us. If they do, great. If they don't—ouch. But, we must always understand that our loving them will NOT make them love us back. And that is the hardest thing for most to grasp. When a person does not love us back, they will less likely have the connection to us or the relationship to make the relationship or connection a viable, much less a meaningful or beautiful one.

I have both been through it personally and experienced it with clients, friends, students, and family members. It is hard to believe much less accept the possibility or reality that we could deeply love someone who does not love us back. But it is important to accept that reality <u>before</u> we choose partners and engage in relationships. Innerstanding that reality will help us to be more discerning as we approach the potentials and minimize our disappointment and disenchantment with our experiences with love. Love is not automatically reciprocal and the fact that it is not returned may not stop us from loving that person-especially when the love we have is either real or grounded in our issues and dysfunctions. But when we find ourselves, not only loving someone-but staying in a relationship with someone who does not love us back, then two questions must be asked. What would make us love someone who does not love us or reciprocate the love? And why would we want to continue trying to give love to someone who will not love us in return?

The former question can uncover some very key issues about how our life experiences have shaped why and how we define love, how and why we love, and most importantly how and who we choose as our partners. This goes back to the previous chapters about why establishing healthy familial relationships through embracing our legacy is essential. The breakdown of the family has not occurred by osmosis, it is the result of the breakdown of our ability to connect, love, and be intimate in healthy ways. As we destroy our families and family values, we also destroy our children's ability to experience healthy love, connection, intimacy, relationships and marriage in childhood so that they can develop healthy conceptualizations of what love and beautiful relationships and marriages are supposed to look like as adults.

Loving someone, even in and with the unconditional love that parents have for children, does not mean that we must expose or tolerate or remain in connected relationships with those who do not/cannot/will not reciprocate the connection, hence the responsibility that love entails. It is better to be at peace alone then in the destructive

bondage of dysfunctional and/or unfulfilling relationships. So sometimes, we have to let

go.

However, it is my contention that as more people reach consciousness and begin

to embrace love as the deeply rooted spiritual-first, mental-second, and emotional

connection to another, relationship and marital dynamics will continue to improve. I

know it is ideal, but they have said I am a dreamer and a revolutionary, but if one

embraces that definition while simultaneously embracing a developed spiritual sense of

self, he/she will automatically embrace the charge- that love comes with a responsibility

and accountability that will not look or feel like responsibility and accountability when

one truly loves. What that means is that the man or woman will not hurt another, betray,

deceive, lie, or murder the love and spirit of another under the guise of love, because he

or she will embrace the connection to that person that love brings. He/She will not have

to be threatened to do right, it will be automatic because he/she values and respects the

gift of the connection. And on the converse, when each embraces that love is a divine

gift that is received and given, he/she will understand that when that gift is being given in

vain, it is o.k. to walk away.

The final part of the definition leads to the next chapter; however, as I have

mentioned throughout this chapter and this work, it is important to decipher love from

lust and being "in love" from infatuation, because the physical and emotional factors that

drive the feelings of lust and infatuation always fade, and can always be regenerated by

another. As a matter of fact, seeking that high is what I believe influences infidelity in

relationships. The excitement of getting to know a person, the first phone call, the first date, the first sexual encounter, the first time you tried that "thing," all fade, just like a high. The first high can never be recreated. The elders who have been married for decades always say that love sustains the commitment and relationship. So when all of those other things fade, love is still there. That is because they have not defined love by the materialistic things. It's not about the flowers, the dinners, the jewelry, the movies, the candy. It is not about the sex. It is not about the kissing and hugging and petting, or even about the conversations. As the definition states love guides those things, and those things may be used as an expression of love. But, even when those things are not present, love still exists. Therefore, a couple can sit quietly, stay in the house always, not buy flowers anymore or make love as much and it has no bearing on the way that they feel about one another.

But when people become attracted to the high that lust and infatuation create, they should not equate and or confuse those feelings with love. If they fallaciously believe that those feelings define love, when those feelings subside, which is natural as people get to know and become comfortable with one another, they will believe that the love has died too. They will then continue to seek the excitement of the superficial instead of the enjoying the peace, depth, and stability that real love brings. Those who are attracted to the high can and will never be satisfied with one person because there is no way that the excitement that the newness creates can be sustained for a long period of time. The confused or those who consciously choose that way will continuously seek that high that can only be sustained by engaging with new people. This goes for men who are driven by new sex, to women who expect flowers, dates, candy and immaculate foreplay every day. It's just not a real identification of something that will last. And, it most certainly

does not define love

Chapter 10
What is Making Love?

This will probably be the most idealistic and short chapter in this book. If you, as a reader, have learned anything from the way in which the chapters of this book are structured, you will know where I am going because you will see how the book has been built.

First both men and women must develop the inner self. As Mary J Blige states, "how can I love somebody else, when I can't love myself enough to know...." One cannot love another until he/she has first learned to love self. Then men and women must develop more healthy concepts or gender identity, that is how we define our manhood and womanhood, masculinity and femininity. After which we must put in context and embrace the power of the body, intimacy, and physical connection. We must understand how the hierarchy should govern physical connection. We must then understand and develop a healthy definition, perception, and conceptualization of love. Only then can we actualize love through the physical manifestation of love-"making love."

In the previous chapter, I stated that love as an action is "the art" of expressing a deeply rooted spiritual, mental, and emotional connection in ways that can be measured by the other. Making love is the ultimate expression of love. Making love is FIYA and POWER when it is achieved within the context that is intended for. Society says "making love," I like the term "Manifesting Love." If we go back and reminisce on the chapter on Embracing Your Queendom and Embracing your Kingdom and put that in context and then add to it the conceptualization of love that was outlined in the previous chapter, and then couple that with viewing oneself as a spiritual being then the ingredients are present for a powerful recipe and an even more powerful outcome. I want to just use a fictional story to illustrate how this thing can really manifest.

Jack is divorced and has been through a lot. In his divorce he lost a lot, specifically the woman that he lost. He was so busy searching for that high, that he didn't realize the love and stability he had at home until he lost her. Over the years, he has had to take time to get himself together, get over the anger, the guilt, and take the time to really get to know him. He realized that the searching that he was doing did absolutely nothing for him but lead him to and through a whole bunch of meaningless encounters with women that could never measure to his wife. He became bored with that life and took the last year to just chill. While chilling he read this book...lol.

Jill is the product of an absent father. After her divorce she went to therapy only to find that she has been seeking the love of her father through every relationship that has led to the abandonment that she's known so well. She watched her mother struggle through the heartbreak when her father left and subconsciously or even consciously she hated her father and even hated herself for feeling like his abandonment meant that he chose not to love her too. But therapy has been rewarding for her. She has finally found peace with herself and her life and has found resolve that if she finds love great. But, loving herself is far more important. As a parting gift her therapist gives her this book...lol

On Friday night both Jack and Jill are invited out to a club with their friends. Not in the mood they both decide to just get some carry out and stay in to watch the game.

Jack has had a long day at the office and is just coming back from working out. Jill has thrown on a pair of sweat pants and has a bandana around her hair. The jingle of the door captures Jacks attention as he stands at the counter. He looks back and as she enters, their eyes meet. (Queue the music)

Immediately they know. Jill blushes but can't help but smile as she quickly breaks the gaze and looks down as if she is digging in her purse for her wallet. Jack cannot stop looking at her, and even though Jill knows that she is not at her best, she can feel his energy. As she approaches the counter to place her order, she passes by Jack who steps aside so that she can access the cashier. If air were an energy or electricity the thunder would have roared or the lightening struck as they passed. She places her order quickly and turns around to step aside for the two people who are behind her.

"Hello. How was your day today?." Jack asks.

"Wow. It was good. How was yours?" Jill responds.

"Hell as corny as it sounds, it was good, but it is great now that I am talking to you." "Now any other day I would suck my teeth and roll my eyes at that line" Jill chuckles, "but I feel the same way. My name is Jill and you are?" she extends her hand. "Jack." "You are kidding right?" "Nope. Jack and Jill. It doesn't get any better than that. And if you had told me your name after I told you mine, I wouldn't have believed you either. I didn't know people still named their girls Jill." "Oh, you got jokes?" "Nah…nah…nah." Jack interjects as they both begin to laugh. "I guess I just never thought I'd find the Jill to my Jack." "Well God makes a Jill for every Jack." "Wow…" Jack pauses. "I like that."

The Meeting

The meeting reflects a pure connection, one that is not driven by some outward physical or sexual attraction that comes from what either of them had or didn't have on. They are instantly drawn to each other by an "energy" that if asked to explain it, they probably couldn't. Because they have found peace with themselves, although they were not "looking," they were open to not only receiving but letting that energy breath between them. They did not consciously or unconsciously let mistrust, fear, anger, or resistance stifle or smother the energy. So the initial connection was allowed to occur in a way in which they really, in casual conversation, got a chance to feel each other. Because Jill has connected to her spiritual side and is not working or acting or playing the game based on the way in which she feels Jack will respond, because she is comfortable and honest with the fact that she is ready for a deeper relationship, she is able to invoke Gods will in the conversation, no matter how casual or humorous. Because Jack is also in that place, he is able to appreciate the invocation.

Now this may seem minimal or even corny to most who have not actualized, it is really significant because by making that statement, Jill has revealed something very important about herself- that she believes that God is at the helm and she is open to being Jack's Jill. Jack has also revealed something very important, that he is not afraid and likes that concept.

"What are you doing at the carry out on a Friday night? Shouldn't you be hanging out with your girlfriends?" "It's funny, they asked me to go out tonight, but I just didn't feel like being in that scene. The game comes on tonight so I'm going to chill, eat my food, kick my feet up and root for my team." "What? What team?" "The

Magic." "The Magic?! Oh you're done then." "What do you mean, I'm done?" "Jill Kobe and the Lakers are going to tear them up." "Well that's why I'm rooting for the Magic. I like rooting for the underdog. Why are you not out with your folks or you're your lady." Jill asks peeking around to get a look at Jacks left hand ring finger. "As funny as it is, my boys invited me to the Sports Bar, but I didn't feel like being in all that either. So, I'm just gonna chill like you and watch it at home. And.." He adds extending his left hand. "I am not married and have to girl. I'm not dating anyone and so I don't have that special lady to sit back and watch the game with. Even if I had a lady, I don't know if she would want to sit back and watch the game anyway-except for my Jill." Jill blushes and laughs. "Would you like to watch the game with me Jill?"

The Crossroads

Now earlier on, I gave a similar example about inviting someone over. The difference here is that if both are spiritually grounded the intention and the energy will be completely different. Now that is not to say that the temptation and the sexual energy will not be present, but it will speak to how well grounded each are, and how willing they will be to deny their physical urges for the best and betterment of the relationship. If they understand that love making is the art and expression of a deeply rooted connection, they will ensure that the connection is deeply rooted before they engage, even though the urge may be more than present.

"You know what Jack, I think I'd like that." "Would you like to come to my house. I promise I'll be a perfect gentleman." "If I didn't think you would I wouldn't even think about the offer."

Setting the limits and establishing mutual boundaries

In that short exchange the boundaries are set. Jack ensures Jill that he expects and will try nothing. And Jill expresses her trust in his intentions and her own value system that ensures that he knows that if he was expecting anything else, she wouldn't even consider it.

Needless to say that evening is the beginning of a beautiful relationship. The two commit to getting to know one another in a friendship where there are no others that they are dating and no sex. They do not want to be distracted by outsiders or the physical lures and lust. Although they are intimate they agree that they are not going to engage in any form of sexual encounter until they reach that point. They stand more and more deeply in love. After 7 months of dating on Christmas Day, Jack gives Jill a thin rectangular box. Jill begins to carefully take off the bow and open the wrapping paper anxious at what it could possibly be.

Laughing she looks up at Jack. "What did you get me Jack a handkerchief?" "Yeah, damn. How did you know? You need it to wipe your nose." I got your wiping nose…" Jill laughs as she touches the tip of her nose and then jumps on Jack kissing him in his lips. Straddling him she continues to open the package. She can feel Jack rise underneath of her. "I know you feel that. You gotta stop jumping on me like that."

Ignoring him Jill continues to open her box with the sassy look on her face. Soon enough she cracks open the box and inside are two airplane tickets to St. Lucia. Tears fall from her eyes and she is speechless. She falls off of Jack who sits up to comfort her. "What's wrong baby? Whoa Whoa what's wrong?" "No…" she tries as she swallows trying to regain her composure. "I love you so much." She breaks. Jack rests Jill's head on her chest. "I love you too baby. But, what's wrong." "Nothing. I am happy." "Shit that's happy? You're scaring me." He laughs lightening the situation. Jill grabs jacks face and looks in his eyes. He brushes the tears from her cheeks and looks at her intensely. In his soul, he yearns to love and protect her. She is his everything. "I am so thankful for you." Jill starts. "I never gave up on love in my heart, but I never thought you would ever exist." "I should have scheduled our vacation earlier." "No, no, it's not about the gift, it's you." "I know baby, I just want you to stop crying." Jack kisses Jill passionately and she returns the passion.

Patience

The opportunity to make love never goes anywhere. It does not have to be the goal or the end to every passionate moment or experience. People don't realize that denying that sexual culmination is like boiling water, a heating geyser, a bubbling volcano. The more it builds, the more powerful the experience, not just physically, but emotionally, mentally, and spiritually. Why? Because when the ultimate connection waits until two people, two spirits, two minds, and two hearts are ultimately connected what more can you ask for? What really happens when the deeply rooted connection is already established and the love making becomes a manifestation and expression of that love? Imagine what it could be like when two people who would die for one another, even before experiencing the warmth and comfort of their temples connection, finally manifest love.

It's two o'clock before Jack and Jill reach the oceanfront. Jack had been patiently planning the trip for Jill who worked so hard in all of her endeavors. He yearned to be the man to her. He had it all planned out, he had envisioned this moment in his head. 85 degrees, blue-green calm water, white sand, the smell of ban de soleil on her beautiful brown skin, just feeling her peace. "Ahhh." Jill screams lightly as she looks at the water. She reaches and jumps up on Jack wrapping her legs around him and kissing his nose. "Thank you baby! Thank you baby! Thank you baby!" She sighs kissing him with each chant. "Oh my God, this is so beautiful. Thank you God." She looks up. She slides off of him and rests her back against her back. "This reminds me of India Aries song where she says St. Lucia reminds her that God is alive. Isn't this the most beautiful." "I don't know Jill I think you are God's most beautiful creation." He hands her another gift-a small box.

My Breakdown

(I have to admit to you all that I, Zoe Spencer, have never written a love story with a happy ending. This is my first. At that last sentence I broke down crying. I have never written a love story, love song, poem or anything with a happy ending, because I have never known the happily ever afters that I wish for those who read this book. I have never experienced the beautiful that I know can exist. But, even writing this for the reader gives me hope, that beautiful is possible.)

Jill looks up at Jack perplexed. It looks like a ring box, but it has only been seven months and she just can't imagine what it could be. The thought that this could be the most beautiful moment in her life evades her. As healthy as she is, as much as she loves and trusts Jack, God can't be that good to her. "Open it." Jack prods sensing her confusion. Her knees get weak so she walks over to the lounge chair that is situated under the oversized umbrella and sits down at the edge. She stares at Jack who is now on his knees in front of her. She is speechless as she carefully unwraps the box.

Unwrapping it is nerve wracking for her. Even though she does not expect any rings, her heart beats. Whatever is inside will be beautiful she convinces herself, but what could it be. She gently slides the small case out of the box. She rests it on her lap and looks at Jack for answers. She cannot open the lid. "Jill, I have been through so much in my life. I made a lot of mistakes. But, my mistakes have helped me to grow more than I ever could have if I had never gone through the things that I have gone through. I messed up a good thing with my ex wife, but I understand that where one door opens, if you trust in God another more precious door will open. The biggest thing that I have learned is to never ever let my blessing pass, miss them, give them, or throw them away. I have learned to just be quiet sometimes and let God lead me. When I met you I was on my path. I was NOT expecting or looking for anyone. When you walked in the door, I knew you were going to be my wife. Open the box."

By the end of his confession, Jill's cheeks look as if she has dipped her cheeks in the ocean. "Are you serious?" She asks. "Yes." He responds. She opens the box and in it sits a beautiful diamond engagement ring. "Jill, will you be my wife?" "Yes."

There are no boundaries or time limits on love.

They don't return to the beautiful suite until 1 in the morning. Jill takes off her shoes and prepares to take a shower. "I'm going to get some ice and soda." Jack states.

135

"O.k." Jill quickly pulls out the negligee that she bought just for this occasion. She rushes to take a quick shower and get dressed before Jack returns. Each time she raises her hand, she cannot escape the glisten from the ring that he so carefully picked out just for her. The thought of being his wife is immeasurable. The thought of being able to spend the rest of her life, having and raising children with the man that she loves is immeasurable. The thought of coming home to him every single night is immeasurable. But the time the thoughts finish running through her head, she does not know how she showered, sprayed, and slipped on her long silk gown with no panties. By the time Jack returns, Jill is laid across the bed in her gown. "DAYUM!" Jack states before he can get through the threshold of the door. Her tanned skin, the mango gown and the white down comforter create a vision that he does not want to forget. "Is that for me?" "Yep." He sets the bucket of ice and the soda's down and rushes to the shower. When the door opens, Jill catches the scent of his soap. She gets up with his lotion and begins to lotion his back, kissing him on his neck and back as she rubs.

His key swells underneath of the thick white robe. He turns around without saying a word. She grabs his head and begins to kiss him passionately. With her right hand she unties his robe, with her left she slides the robe off of his shoulders exposing his bare body. She kisses his chest as she lures him to the bed walking backwards slowly. As she reaches the edge of the bed, she turns him around and prompts him to the white down comforter. She lifts her silk gown until her brown thighs are exposed. He looks up at her thighs, sliding her gown up even more so that he can grip her upper thigh. She leans forward kissing him passionately. His fingers leave prints in her thigh while he runs the other through her Rihanna cut. She moves in rhythms on top of him. They

136

moan like musical instruments harmoniously. There is no fear, no reservation…There is only love, each movement guided by love, each kiss guided by love, the touch guided by love. She is pouring on his stomach and it seeps down into his curly hair luring his key to her canal.

He sits up and raises her gown over her head, exposing her beautiful body. Her look, her skin, her scent, her breath has excited him to the point where he feels like he is going to explode. I love you so much Mrs. X. I love you too baby. He turns her around as the explosions begin to pop. Blood races and rushes through both of their bodies before he even reaches the entrance of her canal. They both listen to their own heartbeats in their heads. Jill screams and moans…. "Aaaaaaaaahhhhhh…" as he enters her. The hairs raise over her entire body and she can feel her heart accelerate beyond measure until it feels like she cannot catch her breath. "Ooooooooo ssshhhhhtt" he exhales as his body contracts, abdominal muscles tensing as if he is trying to complete that thousandth crunch. As soon as he enters her, her canal embraces him in rhythms that he cannot resist. With each stroke they can hear angels sing. They embrace eachother with a passion that neither has EVER experienced.

"I love you so much Jill". "I lah….iiiiiieee…Oh my Gah…" "Yeah let it go baby, I got you." "Ahhh…Iiiiiecc…Ah love you…Oh…." "Oh My God Baby! Oh ssshhhhh." Jack mumbles as he buries his face in hers. He opens his eyes and hers is fixated on him. For a moment it looks like panic takes over Jill's face. God ordained this union. They both scream…. "Oh My God, I love you so much!" And they explode giving everything that they had to each other in that one moment.

And that could be you…Hell, or even me!

Chapter 11
Guiding Your Destiny

How powerful it is that our destiny is largely in our hands. How powerful we are as "men and women" that we are not grounded by the inability to "control" our environment, hence shape our life experience. As human beings we have been given the gift of thought, intelligence, rationality, and logic.

We have the capacity to create and build organized civilizations, societies, nations, and to acquire wealth in its many forms because of this capacity. We have the capacity to love and form healthy, nurturing, and supportive relationships, and to express that connection and love in many different forms on many different levels. WE have the capacity to feel on levels that other creatures cannot. We have the capacity to create and then experience rewarding family and social bonds that serve to shape our lives. But most importantly, we have the capacity to have a wonderful existence that is largely free from the animalistic struggles and fears in this life on this earth. This life can set the foundation and create, promote, and/or even reshape the legacy of generations to come- a legacy that can also define what our after life will be. Conversely, we also have the capacity to destroy self, others, love, family, civilization, society, and life simply by the way in which we use the blessings of humanity.

The part of our own destiny that is in our hands is by in large shaped and determined by the decisions that we make-simply. We choose the right partner, we have a beautiful marriage. We waste time on a jerk and marry him/her because we've been with them so long instead of just walking away, we end up with an unfulfilling marriage,

139

family, and life. We decide not to drink because we have to drive home and we get home safely and with our lives in our own hands still. We decide to drink consciously and then drive under the influence- cause an accident and end up in jail. We lose our jobs and our homes and end up in financial and emotional despair. Even in that downward and harsh negative spiral, we gave up control of our lives to the police officer, the judge, the probation officer, our boss, our landlord or mortgage company because of that decision that we made.

In every situation, with every consequence-positive or negative- one, if he/she is honest can usually trace a chain of events that lead to a particular outcome or experience back to either one, or a string of decisions that we either consciously made or made under the influence of something or some circumstance that distorted our clarity. Therefore, it is beautiful that we do have control of our destiny and the decisions that we make, and logical that we would/should make our decisions as rationally and clearly as possible.

The decisions that we make, then- are largely determined by our character- who we are as individuals, how we perceive, how we process, how we look at life and our places in it. Our decision making processes are embedded in our character, they operate like a hand in a glove. They are intricately intertwined and cannot exist independent of the other. Consequently, a cruddy character will make cruddy decisions-simply. If an individual is selfish or narcissistic, he will make selfish or narcissistic decisions. If a person is impulsive, she will make impulsive decisions. It is almost as if he/she cannot do any different because the decisions made come from the person that is. On the converse if a person is well grounded and balanced, he will make well grounded and balanced decisions. So developing our character is essential to determining how we will make decisions, hence how we live our lives and guide our destiny.

Our character is shaped by our experiences. The saying "we are products of our experiences" is absolute. Our experience shapes who we become. Collectively-experiences shape our character because it shapes how we process, perceive, and interact with the world. We input external stimuli and then we use that information to construct and then interact. The more healthy our experiences, the more healthy we become, or the more likely we will develop healthy characters. We cannot express what we have not experienced, because we simply do not know it. So as people, especially adults and parents or even those in power positions or control over or responsibility for others, we have to be mindful of how we shape the experiences of those around us. Just as significantly, we have to be vigilant about how we feed or nourish our "selves" by and through the environments that we place ourselves in.

Our experiences are shaped by our relationship to our external environment and as an adult we have almost complete control over the environments that we place ourselves in. But, as children we are more dependent on our parents or caretakers. Our childhood then is integral to who we become as adults because it lays the experiential foundation for the development of our characters. This 360 degree cycle is repetitive and goes round and round with each component continuing to feed and build off of the other.

As was stated at the beginning of this chapter, we are "largely" in control of our destiny, and we "by in large" control the decisions that we make. The operative word is "largely." Unfortunately, it is not absolute. There are some things-even many- in life that we cannot control; however, we can control the way those things and experiences effect/affect us. We can control how we manage those things that we cannot control, and in such we can minimize the negative impact and maximize the positive outcome of the uncontrollable. This means that we cannot control the environment, we cannot control the being and actions of others, we cannot control the elements or natural occurrences, or even tragedies; but we can control how we mange and how we allow those things to influence our lives and destinies.

We may have been the victim of child abuse. As young children, we cannot control the actions and behaviors of the adults that we are supposed to trust to care for us. We are often stuck in a situation that we cannot escape. But, when we are able through gaining our own physical and spatial independence, we are able to control how we manage our victimization. And how we do that is a matter of choice and decision making. It is a matter or "mind over matter."

Our parents may not apologize. They may never be the parents or even the grandparents that we need them to be. They may never give us closure or explanation. They may not attend counseling with or without us. Hell, they may not even acknowledge what they did. But that is because they are not willing to grow and change. And we may be angry, hurt, depressed about it all-and rightfully so. We may have issues that stem from what they did to us- and rightfully so. We may have issues about their refusal to grow or change; but does their lack of growth, transformation, or closure mean that we should not or cannot make our lives better? There is a cross roads that guiding your destiny creates. And this is something that is key in the work that we must do to actualize. Follow me

There are many instances, as mentioned above, where we have "the right" to think, be and feel what we do, especially when we are the infamous "victim" of something outside of our control. These "some things" can be death, destruction, abuse, betrayal, infidelity and on and on. Sometimes life deals us some really ugly cards that we don't deserve. But, the ugly hand does not stop, destroy, or derail our lives. We do. We do by the way that we manage the hand that we're dealt. If we throw in the cards we die. If we give up, we lose the game. If we play haphazardly because we don't care, we lose the game. But, if we manage and strategize and become active in trying to reshape our hands, we always have hope for a better hand if we keep playing we might even win.

Guiding our own destiny creates the crossroads of quitting, giving up, or further destroying our lives, (based on the hand someone else dealt), or taking a path that will allow us to "bounce back" from our situations and live a beautiful rest of our lives. Going back to the example, the crossroad that is presented is simple. Do you allow those who hurt you directly to continue to hurt you indirectly through your own actions toward your own self-that you commit in their names? I am an alcoholic in the name of my abusive mother. Do you allow them to continue to control your destiny even when you have the power and capacity to guide it for self? I will not get better in the name of my abusive step father. What does this mean? Your parent may have abused you as a child. When you gain the control to guide your own destiny, do you use your victimization as an excuse to make counterproductive or even fucked up decisions about your own life, or do you strive to ensure that their destiny does not become yours? Do you eradicate the negative influence by displacing or replacing them with positive ones? Do you eradicate the trials and tribulations by overcoming them? Do you regain your power by winning back your life?

Do you become a bully in school? Drop out? Get expelled? Start smoking, or drinking, or using drugs to cope? Do you abuse others? Do you allow your parent's anger to become your anger and thus destroy your own life because of your parent? Do you allow your mistrust for your parents to make you mistrust anyone who tries to get close to you? Or do you do what you need to do to survive the situation that you cannot control with as much of your "self" intact, and then when you gain or regain control work to ensure that the impact of the trauma does not continue to traumatize you and influence you for the rest of your life. Do you find some constructive activity that keeps you out of the house? Do good in school so that you can get a scholarship and go far away to college? Do you seek a healthy and supportive relationship with people who will truly have your back in a positive way?

As an adult, we have the greater part of the capacity to guide our destiny through the decisions that we make. We have the capacity to put our issues into perspective and store them in a place that will allow us to draw the positive, the lessons, the memories from them and use them to not only help ourselves to grow, but to even help others. If we choose to use our bad experiences as excuses to stay stagnant, deteriorate, or even die instead of growing, we have to admit that too. But at some point, even with the death of a loved one, we have to stop living in the emotion of the loss, issue, experience, or trauma and move on. At some point it stops being our parents fault, our fault, or exes fault, or even Gods fault for our continued "stuck" and it becomes our own fault for continuing to allow circumstances outside of us to control our destiny.

We must all understand that the past does not define the future unless WE allow it to. Being who we are today does not mean that we have to stay that "same person" tomorrow or even the moment or second after we feel, see, seek the need for change or transformation. The mistakes we've made, the poor decisions that we've made, the traumas we've had, or even the mediocre life that we've lived, does not have to be the foundation for the rest of our lives. Through guiding our destiny, we have to understand and embrace the power that we always have to guide our destiny- the path to our afterlife.

The question has to be who do we want to be? What do we want to do? How do we want to live? What types of relationships do we want to forge? What do we want to see and how do we want to feel when we get to our golden years and look back on our lives? And most significantly, how do we want to be remembered? What type of mark do we want to leave in/for/on our families, communities, societies, or even this world? What type of legacy do we want to leave?

This life lesson is also key to relationships. Guide your destiny by being accountable for the decisions you make with regards to your relationships. Take responsibility for your own happiness and guide the outcome of your relationships by guiding the input. Do the work on self so that the cycle, the 360 degrees, can be a healthy cycle that promotes beauty, peace, and love in your relationships and in your life. Here is how.

Chapter 12
Self Evaluation / Self Reflection

Now that the foundation is laid, the question is how can we reach beautiful? How do we accomplish reaching actualization or developing and balancing our four states of being without seminars, courses, or even therapy? Of course it may not be as simple as reading a book, unless people have a foundation and a guide of how to actually carry out the suggestions. This chapter is dedicated to helping those who wish to reach higher levels of consciousness, actualization, and balance.

In my coursework, it is always an assignment for my students to keep a journal, so that they can complete the reflection and evaluation assignments. So before you begin this chapter, get a journal. It can be any kind from an actual journal to a notebook. But, it should be a journal that is dedicated completely to your journey toward reflection, evaluation, and actualization...

The key to truly reaching actualization and or reaching the development and balance of the four states is being honest with oneself. The assignments may seem superficial or thera-py, but they are necessary and have very distinct purposes and organization. More importantly, some may think that being honest with oneself is easy, but it is not. It is probably one of the most difficult things to do because we are conditioned to avoid accountability through blame, and ego discomfort through projection. We are trained to believe that everything must be good and healthy in order for us to be good and healthy, and that having experienced anything bad or dysfunctional makes us bad people. But, it doesn't. We may even make mistakes of our own, but even that does not make us bad people, or mean that we do not have the capacity to invoke change and promote transformation in our lives. Truth of the matter is, story be told truthfully, most people experience and/or have experienced some form of dysfunction at some level-some far more than others.

Unfortunately in order to handle, cope with, survive or escape the discomfort of the anger, sorrow, depression, guilt, betrayal, mistrust and all of the other issues and emotions that dysfunction and/or trauma breeds, we often times use what Freud terms "ego defense" mechanisms to do so. Ego defense mechanisms are the attitudes and behaviors that people adapt to protect the ego, or the conscious mind-which is considered an integral part of the self, from discomfort. The most common ego defense mechanisms include rationalization-irrationally justifying what you did- the price of the candy was too high so I stole it, *projection*- projecting your anger or issues onto someone else, you made me hit you, *regression*- moving into an earlier state of development to justify ones actions- 29 year old Joy pulls a temper tantrum and cries like a child when her boyfriend does not buy her the ring she wants, *repression*-pushing an experience into ones subconscious, *denial*- not believing or acknowledging ones actions, or an event, "I saw your girl cheating." No you didn't, *displacement*- diverting emotions to one other than the intended- you had a rough day at work and you are pissed at your boss, but you can't be angry at him, so you come home and yell at your children, and *intellectualization*-trying to create rational and/or intellectual excuses for one's action- I did not pay my taxes because the government is an oppressive system. It is taxation without representation. So the key to reaching self actualization will involve being able to deal with and manage the discomfort that being honest with oneself can sometimes bring.

PLEASE NOTE*It is advised that if anyone has been through extremely stressful or traumatic experiences that he/she not attempt to do the work alone, but seek the help of a professional that can both monitor and guide the process of first resolving internal psycho-social issues and then helping the individual to move toward actualization. Seek a life coach, social worker, psycho therapist, or a psychologist.*

JOURNAL ENTRY ONE: SO TELL ME ABOUT YOUR CHILDHOOD

I remember being in the Masters Program in Social Work at Howard University. The curriculum was not only aimed at helping us to do thorough client assessments, but it encouraged us to do our own self evaluation. In hindsight I support how valuable it is for those who pursue helping professions, especially in the therapeutic or counseling fields, to do their work first. It is essential to avoiding counter transference issues and to being able to build trusting and healthy relationships with clients.

In the assessment and psycho-social development courses and even as it is over-represented in movies, the key was analyzing the childhood of the client. I used to hate this superficial approach and question, well into my practice.

The phrase, "So tell me about your childhood" had been minimized through its overuse and presentation in the media. However, even I, as a therapist, did not realize how significant our childhood is to our adult experiences until I went to therapy myself after my divorce. I realized that my independence and lack of trust and patience in and with relationships stemmed from my issues with my father and my adhesion to my mothers values and presentation as a child. It took Dr. Dorothy Toffolo to teach me that, so that I could then focus more on it in my own practice. So this is probably the most important foundation that can be laid in the quest for self reflection and self evaluation.

Reflecting on and defining the types of relationships that we had with our primary caretakers is essential to uncovering subconscious issues that manifest themselves

148

repetitively in the way in which we choose partners and engage in relationships. An example of it is this. If a male did not have a father figure, or was reared in a household where he witnessed his father cheat on or abuse his mother, it will not only shape how he views manhood and masculinity, but it will shape his perceptions of relationships and women. From that perception, he will develop means of interacting. His mother stays so he views infidelity as a natural and acceptable part of relationships. His mother did not stand up for herself, so he views women as being weak.

Another more common example is a young lady is the product of a relationship that did not work out. She sporadically sees her father. He makes promises to provide and spend time with her, but he never shows up, leaving her consistently disappointed. This affects her perception of self and her perception of what it takes for a man to love her. She has abandonment issues and either detaches herself from relationships or seeks to win the love from men that she could not win from her father, leading to detached or promiscuous relationships.

In this assignment the more deeply one tells the story of his/her childhood, the more comprehensive the information will be for each to evaluate and reflect upon. The beautiful thing about this assignment is that no one has to look at it or read it, but you. You can choose to share with someone or even form a trust circle with those who are growing with you. If you choose therapy as well, it is a good tool to guide your sessions and growth with your therapist or life coach.

However, as mentioned above, please remember that being honest, recollecting, thinking and doing the work is required if you are truly going to be able to make the connections that allow you to figure you out. This is the part of doing what I call "the work" that means that many of us will have to let go of the façade of what our families may have looked like to others and deal with the reality of what they actually were. Or even the part where we realize that we weren't the children or adolescents that we were supposed to be or could have been and it wasn't our parents fault, it was just that we were assholes who didn't listen. Whatever the case, we have to be thorough in recalling the information and as an adult using our adult logic to give a concrete analysis without using the defense mechanisms such as denial, rationalization, or repression to continue to protect ourselves.

Once you have written the story, you can revisit the story with the goal of picking out the breaks, traumas, stressors, dysfunctions, and disconnections that may exist. The next assignment is to write them down. If your father wasn't present, write down absent father, as an example. If your mom was too strict, write down strict mom. If you were the victim of some form of emotional, psychological, sexual abuse, write down abused. If your parents have been happily married for 30 years but your mom or dad were cheating for 29, write it down. If you had present/absent parents, that is parents who were present physically but absent emotionally, write it down. All of these factors, even the smallest ones that may otherwise seem irrelevant become pieces to the puzzles of who we are. These become the foundation and keys to what will come later.

JOURNAL ENTRY TWO: WHAT ARE YOUR WEAKNESSES?

Now this is the section that will not only question and analyze family and childhood experiences honestly; but, this section requires you to do a critical self analysis. Critical means that you focus more on the weaknesses than the strengths, to be able to look at your "self"- which includes your attitudes, behaviors, habits, ways, actions, ways of processing, your level of connection, and your perception of self and the way YOU treat others objectively and critically. As an example, if you were an outsider who was charged with looking at You and Your life and critiquing it, what would you see?

This is probably the most difficult work, because this is the point where you strip all cover off of your ego and find that you are not as tight as you thought you were. All of us who are striving for actualization have had to do this very hard work, and at times it can get really ugly. Nobody likes you and you don't have any girlfriends. You say it's because you hate and don't trust women; but the reality is that they hate and don't trust you. Why? You say everyone thinks you're mean, and you think that is a good thing. But, they don't hate you and think that for no reason. The question for self analysis is what's the reason? Do you have a funky energy? Do you rarely smile? Do you wear the fact that you hate women all over you, so you prevent cool sisters from getting close to you? Are you a boyfriend stealer and a narcissist so you don't trust other women around your man, because you know what you'd do?

You think you are fly man or woman. You spend your last dollar on designer or in clothes. When people are around you all you do is brag about what you got. You think everybody is hating on you because they are jealous of you. But, the reality is that

151

you are a braggadocios wanna-be that has ABSOLUTELY nothing to offer any one outside of yourself but your bragging. You are superficial and have no depth, so you buy the expensive cars, and clothes, or join sororities and fraternities to give you something to hold on to. But, people don't want to hear that shit all the time. Their worlds don't revolve around what you bought or got or have or are getting. And just because they don't want to sit an applaud you while you flaunt your NOTHINGNESS, doesn't make them a hater, nor does it validate your emptiness. You are just superficial and materialistic and nobody likes you.

You are the one who finds fault in everything and everybody. In the therapeutic world, you are called the eternal pessimist. Your negative energy adorns you like a cloak and crown. When you walk in a room in starts raining. The only time you get energy is when you are discussing someone else's demise, so the only people that tolerate you are the ones who share your negativity. Because of your negative energy, nothing positive ever happens. But, for you it's not your fault, it is the world's fault because the world owes you something.

These are some common examples, but there are more. This self analysis is crucial because it is only until we begin to define how our energy and what and how we are, act, behave influences our interaction that we can begin to make changes in our own lives that will improve the quality of our interaction and relationships with others. I have always been taught and believe that the truth is the truth even if we don't acknowledge the truth. When we consistently find ourselves in the same or similar situations, experience, relationships dynamics at some point we have to stop pointing at and blaming others and begin to look at, who? Self!

Ultimately, aside from acts of nature or acts of God, the adage that we are products of our experiences, and our lives are defined by the decisions WE MAKE is so deeply profound, yet so simple. So, if this is true, the key to changing our experiences, does not involve changing the world to suit our limitations, weaknesses, dysfunctions, attitudes, behaviors, perceptions etc, but it involves changing our selves so that we get a better experience out of life.

JOURNAL ENTRY THREE: DEFINE WHAT YOU DESIRE OUT OF A RELATIONSHIP AND MARRIAGE (DEFINE YOUR IDEAL RELATIONSHIP AND MARRIAGE). ON A SEPARATE PAGE DEFINE YOUR IDEAL PARTNER. DEFINE THE CHARACTERISTICS OF THE LAST THREE PEOPLE THAT YOU HAVE DATED. ASSESS HOW THEY FIT.

In this assignment, you are being asked to delve deep and venture to be corny in identifying what you desire from a relationship. Again the key is to be honest and real with yourself. As mentioned in earlier chapters, one of the problems is that women especially try to play the game like men. Here is your chance, both men and women, to create, write down, and actually conceptualize what you want out of a relationship. This assignment is crucial because it forces one to actually think about, or even plan, what they want from a relationship. This will allow you to then conceptualize it once it has been constructed. When a person is able to actually conceptualize and has actually laid down a plan, it is less likely that he or she will be lured into impulsive or counterproductive decision making when it comes to relationships.

The second part of this assignment is also crucial. On a separate page, you will have to write down the characteristics of the ideal partner. Ideally, this should be done by writing down the physical ideal, emotional ideal, mental ideal, and spiritual ideal. This also allows a person to first think about, define, write down, and then conceptualize that ideal partner.

The next assignment is to define the characteristics of the last three relationships that you have had.

Now the final phase of this assignment which is the assessment is key. The assessment involves assessing what you have created and conceptualized as your ideals and then to compare and contrast how the ideals fit to the actual. The goal is to see and analyze how the two either fit or contradict one another. Let me give you a prime example.

Let's say that I have identified my ideal relationship as one that is mutual and reciprocal, trusting, monogamous, committed, lively and exciting, spiritually grounded, and real. My ideal partner is honest, spiritually grounded, poetic, conscious, adventurous, enjoys travel and sports, not afraid of and ready for commitment, secure-emotionally, mentally, and financially, faithful, funny, giving, and loving. Now these are my ideals, and they sound good and the match- that is fit nicely together. They are complimentary. But watch this. The contradictions come out when I begin to evaluate my last relationships and my last three partners/dates/boyfriends etc.

When I do the analysis, I have written down that I have met my last two boyfriends at the club. They never went to church or any religious or spiritual institution in the year that we dated. My first, Mike was so sexy. He was tall, dark, black hair, well

154

dressed. Fine. I also met Tony at the club. I am always meeting guys at the club and bar, because that's where I go to find him. Mike used to be the man in the club, all the girls wanted him. He had a fly car and always had women. We started off friends, he used to have a lot of women and I told him that I wasn't going to deal with that. So we were friends for the first few months and then we got together. I did everything for him and he did nothing. In analyzing him, he was selfish, he lied, I caught him cheating, he didn't support me, and acted like He was doing me a favor by being with me. But, I loved him.

Now there is the huge contradiction, the guys that I choose to date and even the way that I meet them has absolutely no relation to my ideal. NONE! I say I want a spiritually grounded man, but even if I said a Christian man, I don't go to church to meet them. I don't ask and no nothing about their spiritual or religious beliefs. The guys I meet are regulars at the club and bar. They are the big ballers that always have a lot of women around because they are sexy. They were dating when I met them and did not automatically commit to me. I find that the way I go about seeking and choosing a partner is completely counterproductive to what I really want.

Now generally if one wants a trusting relationship then he/she has to choose a trustworthy partner. If one wants an honest relationship, he/she must chose an honest partner. If he/she wants a spiritually grounded or religious partner, we can't expect that we will likely find him in the club drinking, womanizing etc. Do you get it?

JOURNAL ENTRY FOUR: DEFINE LOVE

I gave my definition of love in this book. But, I think that it is important for each reader to define what love means to and for them-to conceptualize their idea of love.

155

Again once we conceptualize our ideas we can begin to develop strategies to reach our goals. As these assignments progress the end will allow each person who has completed the journey to put the pieces of their own puzzles together, to find individualized answers to the obstacles in their lives and relationships and begin to develop ideals that are true to their desires and expectations.

JOURNAL ENTRY FIVE: DEFINE YOUR BEAUTIFUL

This entry is designed to encourage the participants to define the beautiful qualities and characteristics of self. The goal is to identify the beautiful parts of your self that people do not see looking at you. I am not just talking about the beauty mark on your back, although I encourage you to include the physical, but more importantly the beautiful parts of your emotional, mental/intellectual, and spiritual parts about yourself, and even your material and physical assets. These are the things that you would bring to a relationship to make it and your partner adore you.

Many times, people think that it is all about giving in a relationship and that receiving appreciation is supposed to come secondary or not at all. Knowing what you bring to the table and appreciating your own self worth and potential in a relationship is key to ensuring that others seek, acknowledge, but most importantly appreciate those things as well.

JOURNAL ENTRY SIX: DEFINE MAKING LOVE AND THE CHARACTERISTICS OF THE PERSON THAT YOU WILL MAKE LOVE TO.

If you are a virgin, place this step after the next. Now it's your turn to do the infamous assignment that led to the creation of this book. Based on your definition of love, define making love and then conceptualize the characteristics of the person that you would make love to. In this definition and conceptualization include what type of person your beloved will be and what type relationship you would have to be in for making love to occur.

JOURNAL ENTRY SEVEN: DEFINE YOUR IDEAL MARRIAGE: WHAT ARE THE CORE CHARACTERISTICS THAT YOU BELIEVE YOUR MARRIAGE WILL HAVE TO HAVE TO LAST "TIL DEATH DO US PART."

This last assignment reflects the happily ever after, which is just a new beginning, the journey into the next chapter, the next level of a relationship. Unlike the fairy tales, the story does not end with marriage and it does not exist happily ever after until death do you part. It, just like the relationship, requires work, patience, and growth. All of the steps before create the foundation for a healthy marriage because having a happy and beautiful marriage is based on the foundation laid during the dating process. Marriage is not an empty goal that is detached from our interactive, relational, and dating experience. It is grounded in it.

Far too many people think that marriage and even having children are going to bring people closer together, restructure, reshape, change, or transform the nature of the relationship. If the relationship is fucked up before you get married, it will most likely be fucked up when you do. If the marriage is fucked up before you have children, the additional stress and responsibility and detraction that children bring (as beautiful as they are), it will probably be more fucked up when they get here. That is unless people consciously see the need for change and commit to making it better, and then make the changes necessary to make it work. But, most often when a relationship starts on shaky ground, it remains on shaky ground until that final earthquake comes and the foundation crumbles. Although some may argue the exceptions, the exceptions come too far and few between to even be significant. So, they might as well be discounted to deter those who consider it from going against the odds.

So if you truly desire marriage and family, especially a beautiful marriage and family, starting here with strengthening, reassuring, or even redefining how you operate within the dating and interaction scene is key. Doing this involves being able to get as close to your "self" and getting to know your "self" as deeply as possible. This means that each of us must stop allowing other people and things outside of us dictate who we are, but more importantly who we become.

Chapter 13
Making It Beautiful: What It Takes

There are many arguments about what it takes to make a marriage beautiful. When I was going through my own divorce, I remember being hyper vigilant about older couples. I used to, and it seems like it was so common during my struggle, see so many older couples out engaging, walking, holding hands. I used to look at their faces and just see a sense of comfort, connection, and peace. I used to always think that there was this magic formula. But, I realized that people my grandparents age just stayed married. I couldn't tell if it was the time or what. So, I got into the habit of asking older couples how long they had been married, 30, 40, 50 years-as long and longer than I had even been on this earth. It was and remains amazing.

So, I decided to ask my Uncle Robert and Aunt Alice, who had been married almost 50 years before my Uncle Robert passed. When I sat down, I thought I was going to hear some happily ever after story. The first thing that they said is that "it was work." They told me "off the break" that it wasn't easy. Not that it was difficult, but what they were saying was that my magic dust dream was not actual. At the core they agreed that it was the love and commitment that they had to one another. After that discussion, I would ask other older couples and even young couples who had been married more than 10 years, what it takes. I needed to know for my own purposes because I wanted/want to do it right the next time. I wanted to also understand what I didn't have in my own marriage that successful marriages had. And in all of the discussions that I have had there has been one common theme, "it is not easy, it is work" but we are "committed."

But, in my own mind as I do, it didn't quite fit. I understood but it didn't fit. I loved my ex husband. As a matter of fact, I knew a lot of people who loved and got married and then got divorced-painfully. So, I didn't get it. So, for many years I was trying to find the answer, trying to understand the puzzle of what it takes to make it beautiful. And ironically, as it has most often been, I did not find an answer that made me exhale until I was teaching my Marriage and the Family Class at Cheyney University. It's funny how teaching and learning really go hand in hand.

I realized that it wasn't love that guided the success of relationships and marriages. Just as everyone had been saying it was commitment. But, that was the key. What does commitment really mean and what does it really entail? Plenty people make commitments but it just doesn't work out. So what was the difference between those who break up, leave, abandon, divorce- and those who stay together not just miserably, but those who stay together and not only make it work, but make it beautiful?

A commitment can be made verbally but the mere nature of relationships in today's era shows that that is not enough. People enter into commitments without commitment to the commitment. Like love, people enter it conditionally. Aside from the most unconditional love between parent and child and vice versa, people will love until somebody does something that we don't like or ceases to be what we want them to be. ON the converse, people say they love, but they will do things to hurt the other. So the difference between those who make it beautiful and those who don't really involves the understanding and conceptualization of commitment.

Like love, commitment cannot be conditional if a couple wishes to make it beautiful "until death do us part." But too often it is. People commit until somebody makes them mad and then they leave. They get married, take the ultimate vow of commitment to not only each other but to God, and then as soon as something happens- worse, poor, sickness or whatever, they run for divorce. Equally people make a commitment but then breach the commitment through infidelity, adultery, betrayal, and dishonesty. What I realized is that in relationships and marriages the commitment to the relationship has to be two things- mutual and unconditional. Further what I realized is that the keys to making it work weren't the ideal terms that are at the top of our lists like honesty, trust, fidelity, connection, respect etc.; but those things come out of what I have termed the 4 C's and L. The 4 C's are: Commitment, Communication, Conflict Resolution, and Compromise. And the L, of course, is Love.

Commitment

Like so many other mantras, quotes, phrases, vows, society minimizes the marriage vows by joking, plastering, defiling, and deconstructing them-specifically in the media in its various forms. In such, people have become desensitized to what it really means and entails. In planning weddings and marriages, we become so consumed by the material and superficial of the "pomp and circumstance" of a ceremony and reception that only lasts a day, that we forget about what all of the "pomp and circumstance" represents. It represents the what? "Commitment!"

I don't know how many Judge Judy's, Milian's, Karen's, and Mathis' that I have seen where people are suing over photographs, dresses, limousines, and caterers. And I don't know how many Divorce Court shows I have flipped through that demonstrate that the marriages were beyond foundationless and doomed from the start. It is so crazy because all of those things are NOT what the marriage is about.

That fairy tale wedding is like a high, and without foundation the subsequent marriage will be the ultimate crash if people are not aware. Those things become beautiful when the couple and the union is bound by love-that deeply rooted spiritual, mental, and emotional connection between two people. The energy from that love should be the driving force behind any "ceremonious" marriage. But, even in the ceremony people have to stop being so desensitized about the actual commitment.

Although there are many variations, I want to use the traditional Christian wedding vows as an example. Here is one of the most common. Let's break it down.

"I, Jack, take you Jill, to be my wedded wife/husband. To have and to hold, from this day forward, for better, for worse, for richer, for poorer, in sickness or in health, to love and to cherish 'till death do us part. And hereto I pledge you my faithfulness."

Now let's put it in its appropriate ceremonial contexts. This is not a play or a show it is a marriage. The bridesmaids and groomsmen and guests are not an audience to this performance, they are witnesses to not only this union but to the exchange of vows. They are supposed to be a part of ensuring that they too support this union. In earlier years, it was even customary for them to also commit to supporting the union. The bride, groom are not actors or performers, and the pastor is not the director or conductor-although the hoopla may make is seem so. They are two people who are making a commitment to one another and to God before their witnesses. The vows that are spoken or recited are guided by the Pastor or Priests, who serve as the religious figure or "servant of God." So this is not just some production, no matter how big it is, it is the most integral part of the marriage.

It is the part of the marriage where the ultimate verbal commitment, that is supposed to guide the physical, emotional, mental, and spiritual commitment is made.

Now, many will flop through the vows with no emotional, mental, much less spiritual connection to them. But, let's analyze this short passage from a spiritual and mental perspective for one second. First, each are asked do they take one another as their "wedded" wives or husbands. The term "wedded" reflects a holy bond. So even the beginning establishes the commitment to the bond between the two.

Now the part that we all know and have become desensitized to is probably the most important. This is what my Uncle Robert and Aunt Alice and all of the countless couples who commit really get, and those of us who have taken the vows haphazardly, including my ex and I, did not get. And I admit it. I did not get it when I got married. *"To have and to hold, from this day forward, for better, for worse, for richer, for poorer, in sickness or in health, to love and to cherish 'till death do us part."*
"To have and to hold from this day forward means committing to, for the lack of a better word, the possession, respect, protection, and accountability to and for the other. I will "have you" and "hold you." When one says these words, they are committing to giving themselves to the other- I give myself to you and allow you to hold me. You become *My* wife and I become *Your* husband-and vice versa from *this* point forward.

Now watch this…and feel it in its spiritual and intended context. You see these words are deep, really, really deep. I get excited hear because I finally get it and it is really deep. It's not something that one would say, recite, or repeat lightly if they took it literally, as it is intended. But, the problem is people do not take their vows literally, they do not take the commitment literally. For most divorce is a livable consequence of not honoring the vows. There is no immeasurable consequence. But, these vows are not to be recited, and the marriage is not to be entered into lightly, the commitment is not to be entered into lightly. If one would die the moment they ceased to honor the vow, people would not take the vow or enter into the institution of marriage lightly.

So far it says that two people will be spiritually bound to one another under the eyes of God and before witnesses. They vow to give themselves and "hold" one another. And urban culture, when someone says "I'm gonna *hold* you. I'm going to *hold* it down," that means something- deep. It means that the person can be depended upon without question from this day forward. But then wait, the vows don't stop there, they go on to say that they will have and hold from this day forward *for better or worse, for richer or poorer, in sickness and in health UNTIL __DEATH__ do us part.* It doesn't and can't get any clearer than that! All circumstances are accounted for in the first part of "for better or worse" that means it doesn't matter what happens whether you are happy or sad, angry or glad, excited or bored, you made the commitment UNTIL DEATH, so it doesn't matter. But, you didn't feel it though. It doesn't matter! It doesn't matter how you feel, it doesn't matter whether you are struggling financially or not, it doesn't matter whether you "fall out of love" or not, it doesn't matter if you get fat or he gets bald, you made the commitment until death. No differences are irreconcilable according to the vows. And then finally, both vow to be faithful each to the other, and faithful is not just a sexual faithful, it is a physical, emotional, mental, and spiritual faithful- not only to the other, but also to the WILL OF GOD. What did you say! DAMMIT! It doesn't get any clearer than that.

Now many people are rationalizing these assertions, just like they rationalize the impending divorce. Well if it doesn't work, God doesn't intend for me to be miserable for the rest of my life. You are right. (And so am I because this is exactly what I did and said to myself. It is exactly what I prayed about.) And the truth is He (God) probably didn't intend for you (me) to marry that person and take that vow either. He probably showed you all kinds of signs before you took that plunge and you did it anyway under the intellectualization that "if it doesn't work we can get a divorce." That is what I did. Well as was mentioned earlier, it wasn't working before you got married, why didn't you just walk away then? Why did you have to wait until you spent money, involved everyone else, bought property together, and even had children to expose them to a dysfunction and a weight that could have been cut off with minimal pain many years ago? Why would you commit to a broken being before God if you had reservation about your ability to keep your promise to one another and to God before you made the commitment? The commitment was optional. You didn't have to make it.

Even as significantly to those who commit to bring life into this world. Why commit to bringing a child into a dysfunctional relationship or marriage. Why use a child as the wrench or screwdriver that you convince yourself will fix your relationship, tighten the bond of your marriage? Marriage, commitment, childbearing are all conscious decisions that we make. As mentioned in the last chapter, they are decisions that not only influence our own destiny, but ultimately influence the experience of our children. If we can't be true to self, can't we at least be true to the children that we are responsible for and can't we just as significantly be true to God.

Now this is the point about the beauty of commitment and the significance about analyzing the vows. On all ends, if a person really took the vows and the ceremony of marriage literally, we would make better decisions about the people that we choose and

165

how we build our relationships. We would not be as nonchalant about making commitments that we know we cannot, or one or the other will be least likely to honor.

The commitment is the MOST integral part of marriage. It supersedes love and guides love. It can even make a relationship work without love or encourage love to blossom within its confines. That is why arranged marriages are successful. But as stated it must contain two essential components. It must be mutual and unconditional. The premise of this work that we cannot change or control others is key to this premise. We cannot make a person love us, we cannot make a person faithful to us, we cannot make a person commit to us. Those things, just like they are for us, are choices. And we cannot make a person choose in our favor. So understanding where and being honest about where people are with us is not an option, it is necessary. Both must be committed to the union. My ex was not. If one person is not committed and does not get there, the union is doomed to at best mediocrity. This one dimensional entry into marriage leads to the "God does not intend for me to remain in this unhappy and unfulfilled." But if you believe that marriage must be until death, then you would be more hesitant to enter into a half yoked marriage.

On the converse, when two people are committed, the commitment to each other guides everything. Love, that deeply rooted connection, can and should be the foundation for one's intent and commitment to the other because a commitment that grows from love will make the commitment stronger and more beautiful. But, when two people are committed, especially in marriage, and truly believe that they will have to be together for the rest of their lives, it's like being handcuffed. You are essentially bound to the other for the rest of your life. Consequently, you are not going to do anything to

166

destroy or disturb the connection, and you are certainly not going to do anything to hurt the other person because you are bound to them. So, hurting them would be either hurting, or adding a burden to your own self. If you injure them you will have to carry the weight of that. If you murder their spirit you will have to drag it along and have it affect your own until the end. So to avoid that, each will take care of the other to avoid that because they know that not to will disrupt and bring angst to the rest of their lives.

Here is an example. Many married couples are confronted with the opportunity to commit adultery, to be unfaithful emotionally or physically, during the course of their marriage. Now those who think physically, are impulsive decision makers, or those who have not embraced the commitment will be more easily swayed. Those who think spiritually, are rational and processing decision makers, and especially those who are committed to their marriage will have an easy time making the decision. Although it is always a matter of whether or not one will get caught and then a matter of conscience, these consequences sit at the helm of the boat. To get caught or to betray the trust and respect of one's husband or wife, poses the possibility of causing severe problems in and destroying the fiber of the marriage. If divorce were not an option, the person would have to live in a marriage with the weight of the adultery on his/her head until he/she died. So in order to find peace and balance and even happiness in the marriage, he/she would have to go through a lot to restore the marriage to its original state. So, in processing and understanding the commitment, the temporary excitement of experiencing something new wouldn't be worth destroying the stability, peace, balance and foundation of the marriage. See it?

Even more lightly, each would be committed to keeping the other happy and satisfied, because he was sure with self before entering the marriage, so it would always be about what is best for the family, which would include both partners. This is the beautiful that can be created in a marriage. This is what leads to the peace on the faces of the elders who have been married for 50 years. This is the key to marital satisfaction and longevity- a commitment that is born out of love.

Communication

As mentioned in the first two chapters, being able to develop and utilize solid communication skills is key, even before the marriage. This is something that people in this world must develop. It is core to understanding, perception, and then conflict resolution and compromise. And I would argue it is one of the most underdeveloped skills. Especially in this technological era, we are enabled by the ability to use passive aggressive communication styles and means. We can text our issues without dealing with confrontation of our emotions or the emotions of others. We use email, where we do not have to actively communicate to communicate and resolve conflict. We respond or fail to respond, we say what we would never say face to face, we yell when we are not yelling, and we cut off communication at will. On the converse, we fail to communicate at all, instead we just react.

Most trouble in relationships stems from the fact that the couple fails to adequately communicate with one another. Communication is not just a word. It is an action and an interaction that comes in, and encompasses, many forms, that ironically cannot be conveyed through technology. Communication is verbal and non verbal, it is tone and energy, it is visual as well as auditory. And all of those things together shape the interaction that is communication. When one or more parts of the process and interaction are missing, the process of communicating is drastically impeded and/or compromised. Think about it. How many times have texts and emails been misconstrued? I just learned that using all caps was yelling. Hell, how many people have I offended? Is that why they didn't text me back?

We don't even talk on the phone anymore. I used to advocate against communicating important issues and resolving conflicts over the phone, now people will be in the same room texting to resolve conflict. What is that? This is a means to avoidance, another defense mechanism- that is working around an issue so that the individual does not have to engage in the emotion and/or ego discomfort of dealing with it face to face. But it is the face to face contact, the communication that makes people more responsible for active listening, procession, responding, and being accountable for what is said. Technology is like the internet, which has become the nemesis to relationships. It is destroying the fiber of relationships through breaking down the communication process.

Communication is key to building a relationship by allowing both parties to get to truly know one another. Not just getting to know one another by what they say verbally, but being able to gauge mannerisms, detect inconsistencies, and feel the person's energy. One can only learn a person through interaction, physical interaction proximity wise that allows people to experience another. However, communication is critical to conflict resolution.

One must be clear about the issue at hand. He/she must construct his words and presentation to maximize the outcome. He/she must use active listening. He/she must be open to receiving the opinion and views of others. He/she must remove as much of the negative emotion that is attached to the issue as possible, yet he/she must be sensitive and empathetic to the emotion that issues cause. He/she must process the information objectively, and then he/she must develop responses and reactions that are geared toward resolving the conflict and/or reaching compromise. These essential tasks cannot be adequately achieved and should not be attempted through email, text, IM, smoke signal, Facebook walls, blogs, or twitters.

In marriage, communication can never be broken down. It is the core to allowing the commitment to work. If love is a car, and commitment is the key and the ignition, then communication is the gas. You may be in the car (love), you may take the key and turn the ignition (commitment/marriage), but if there is no gas (communication) the car won't start or run.

Conflict Resolution

Conflict resolution speaks for itself. It involves the ability to resolve conflict effectively. As mentioned above, if a couple has developed good communication dynamics, conflict resolution should be very easy. Communication is key to effective conflict resolution. Issues, problems, disagreements are guaranteed 100% to arrive in the marriage. It is human nature. Because two people who may be very close and have very similar and/or completely opposite characteristics that fit together to fuel the love and relationships are still two separate people who will experience some things at different places, perceive some of the same experiences differently, issues and problems occur. It

170

is always an issue of how couples resolve conflict. It involves how well they express the issues and work through them through mutual understanding or compromise.

The most common issue with conflict resolution is exposing "the root" of the problem which is often times masked by a whole host of more superficial, yet easily accessible issues. One thing that must be understood about issues and problems is, if the root of the issue or problem is not addressed in conflict resolution it will continue to manifest, just like a real root. If you pluck a dandelion and leave the root, the dandelion may be gone for a while, but it *will* come back. Why? Because the root is still there. If one looks for a rose bush as the cause of the dandelion problem and plucks the rose bush, the dandelions will continue to be a problem.

What I have seen in relationships the arguments and discord center around issues that are not the root of the problem. Let me give a common example. A husband goes out with his friends for guy's night. He doesn't get home until 4 in the morning. His wife is absolutely livid. He does not understand why she is angry. She jumps on him and they get into an argument. They fail to resolve the issue. The next morning he leaves the toilet seat up and his cereal dish in the sink. His wife calls him and fusses at him telling him how inconsiderate he is. From that point forward the red eye is fixated on his every move. The tension escalates and the husband becomes more frustrated with his wife's behavior. They agree to talk when he gets off from work. She expects him at 6 and he gets home at 7. She tells him he missed his window and shuts down. They agree to come to therapy with me…lol. What is your assessment?

Most men and women will deviate in their assessment of this, with it being a universal gender solidarity on it except for the few secure men and women who will get it. No, coming home at 4 in the morning is not the issue. When it is all uncovered, the issue will generally either be TRUST or perceived and or actual DISRESPECT. Most often when people are "clocking" their spouse's whereabouts and their time, there is an underlying issue of trust. When one trusts his/her partner time and space does not matter. Why would a person be mad otherwise, because it's a disrespectful time? Well perhaps it is. But that can be resolved by setting boundaries. If the boundaries have been set and agreed upon through the mutual process of communication and compromise and that boundary is deliberately crossed, then there is the issue of disrespect. But this is not generally the case.

All of the other issues are manifestations of the original conflict not being resolved. You are not mad about the toilet or the bowl, when all is well you flip the toilet down, put the cap on the toothpaste and put the dish in the dishwasher. If these things were issues they could have easily been resolved by communicating the expectations and reaching a compromise. But, this is generally not the case.

What happens in conflict is people get emotional, on both sides, and seek to have their emotions satisfied instead of the conflict resolved. What does this mean? The most common emotional response to conflict is anger. Anger is one of the most powerful emotions and energies. I liken anger to fire. It seeks to spread and is fed by exposure to the air-to the universe. Fire, like anger, is relentless. Reciprocating negatively, or feeding anger with negative responses, is like gasoline. The negativity literally fuels the anger and can lead to an explosion. So, in managing conflict, all have to be aware of this dynamic and potential in order to minimize any negative outcome.

Because anger is consuming when people get mad, it's not easy to let go. They want people to, in essence, pay for making them mad. So in that case, any interaction and communication that comes behind the anger is most often designed to make the other feel the anger, to express the anger instead of expressing the issue. And in the minds of the angered, either consciously or unconsciously, there is a short list of water, baking soda, or caps that will smother the anger- that is a short list of reactions and/or responses that will make it better.

The problem is that energy oftentimes begets energy. That is why in the communication section being mindful of the delivery was listed as important. When two people are angry the issue and the goal both get lost in the mire of other issues that come up or are born out of the anger. This is where balance between the four states of being come in to play.

One has to be able to call on and utilize the higher states in conflict resolution. Even the mental will allow one to put things into a perspective that allows resolution to occur. Leave it to the lower states and the couple could end up destroying the marriage over a simple issue that could have been resolved simply.

ANGER

"You coming in here at 4 in the morning!" Ohhh..wait. "YOU COMING IN HERE AT 4 IN THE MORNING. YOU MUST BE CRAZY. WHERE THE HELL WERE YOU?" "I told you that I was hanging out with the fellas tonight." "UNTIL 4 IN THE MORNING?!" "Yeah I didn't think it would be an issue." Crossroads. "DON, YOU WEREN'T WITH THE FELLAS UNTIL 4 IN THE MORNING." The accusation leads to anger. "What do you MEAN I wasn't with the fellas, where in the hell would I be?"

173

"I DON'T KNOW WHERE THE HELL YOU WERE. YOU TELL ME?" "I TOLD YOU WHERE I WAS! WHAT DO YOU WANT ME TO SAY, I WAS WITH ANOTHER WOMAN?! YOU NEED TO STOP BEING SO DAMN INSECURE." "OH SO YOU WERE WITH ANOTHER WOMAN? THEN YOU CAN GET YOUR SHIT AND GO BACK." Gets up and starts pulling stuff out of the closet. "WHAT THE HELL ARE YOU DOING? YOU ARE CRAZY! I DIDN'T SAY I WAS WITH ANOTHER WOMAN." "YES YOU DID!"

CONFLICT RESOLUTION:

If the time was an issue, those boundaries could have been set beforehand. What is a respectable time for a married man or woman to be in based on that couples standards. But if they were not, when it started getting late one or both could have called to ask what time, or let the other know what time he/she would be home. If this did not happen, the following will only sound corny if one places the emotion above the goal. "I was waiting for you. I didn't know you would be so late. What happened?" This is a non threatening approach that expresses the person's feelings and opens for response. "We were having so much fun shooting the breeze, I really lost track of time. We were at the pool hall and Mike was....I'm sorry, I should have called you. When I looked at my watch, we were all like oh..oh. So I grabbed my cell to see if you had called." "I didn't want to bother you." (Although sarcastically) "No, you would have put me back in touch with time. I thought you were probably asleep when I didn't see any missed calls. But, I'm sorry baby. Were you worried?" (Non threatening way of bringing out the lack of trust concern.) "No, I just wondered where you were at that hour." "I wouldn't be any where that I wouldn't want you to be. "I'm sorry baby, that won't happen again." "O.k."

Compromise

Compromise is the mutual act of selflessness and conflict resolution. It is what must occur when two people disagree and cannot reach consensus. It is where they put the well being of the union above their own desires. But as stated it *must* be mutual so that it does not become an issue or a burden for one person. It is neither giving in and/or giving up, it is finding a balance, a negotiation that both can consciously relate, accept, and adhere to.

The above situation represents a conflict between two grown adults who are in a peer relationship. In a marriage or even an intimate relationship both partners are equal. The wife is not the mother and the husband is not the child-or vice versa. There is free will in a marriage and that is why commitment is first in this chapter. The commitment to the marriage will govern will and choice if it is truly embraced. There should never be that type of dictatorial or controlling power dynamic in a marriage because it leads to resentment and problems-always.

There has to be a mutual respect and trust that guides the marriage. So, in that situation, it is not up to the woman to tell the husband when to come home and define how his social life will go. But, the fact that it bothered her must not be minimized, ignored, or disregarded by the husband either. There was a disconnect. There was an issue. There was a conflict, and so it must be addressed and resolved so that it doesn't occur again or build.

175

In the scenario, the husband agreed that he lost track of time, which means that he also understood that it could be a point of contention. Only an insecure and selfish man would take the stance that he can come home when he wants to. And only an insecure and selfish woman would take the stance that she must prevent him from going out anymore. These actions come from selfishness and trust issues that have no place in a marriage. So the question is how they will resolve the conflict through communication and conflict resolution.

"Well, you know what we never sat down and discussed how we will handle it when we go out without each other. How do you feel?" "Well I don't care Jill. As long as you are doing right by our marriage as I know you will, when you hang out with your girls, I trust you. But, I do know that if you were out until 4 and didn't call or didn't answer, I would have a problem. So I understand." "Do you think 4 is too late to be coming in the house?" "It depends on what's going on. I don't think it should be done on a regular, but sometimes you know. I think if we are going to be out that late, we should call." "Well I think it's too late." "So what time do you think is good, 3 at the latest." "O.k. I can agree with that." "And if it goes beyond that we should call." "That's a bet." They spoon and go to bed.

I could not leave this chapter without addressing the influence of the infamous "outsiders." These outsiders include family, friends, neighbors, and co-workers. While I believe that support networks are necessary to help individuals to process and work through problems, it takes a very, very well grounded and special person to be able to effectively do that. And those very, very special people come far and few between. So for the most part, I am an advocate of keeping "the outsiders" out of your business.

However, if couples have those special people that they trust, they have to be mindful, no critical, of where these people are in their own spaces. Fellas if your best man told you not to marry her, he should never be the one you discuss issues with your wife with. Ladies, if your girl is single or in a dysfunctional marriage, she should never be the one you share your issues with your husband with. Neither of them will be able to remove themselves from their own experiences to give you good advice.

Parents are equally "iffy." Unless they are the ones who can give you tough love and truly know your wife or husband, talking to them could be shaky. This is because parents are going to usually be protective of their sons and daughters. When things happen, they store it. They are not as forgiving as you may be. When you tell them something that is guided by the way you spin it at the time, their first inclination is going to be to protect you. If you get the spin wrong, you cannot go back and undo it. They have already stored it, and it will most likely shape the way they interpret the situation and feel about your spouse. The more you spin, the more intricate the web you weave in your parents minds, until they lose faith in your marriage. Once they lose faith, it will not come back, especially not as quickly as yours.

Once your support network loses faith in your marriage, there will be increased energy to support confusion, negativity, disregard, and even divorce. Marriage is hard enough without the negativity of the outsiders influencing the way you manage conflict in your marriage.

Lastly, people often ask me about new friends in relationships, so this will be my "perfessional" opinion-that is my personal and professional opinion. I used to say it is o.k. As long as you can bring her or him to the house and they interact with the husbands and wives and become friends of the family, it was o.k. Now I'm not saying that I do not believe that husbands and wives will not meet new people that they connect with on their life journeys, but all have to be honest about the origin of the interaction so that they can be sure they do not set themselves up.

Internet sites and friends. HELL NO!!!NO!!!!NO!!!! Husbands and wives have no business on dating, mingling, chatting, cheating, interactive porn or any other sites that promote emotions, actions, reactions that are or even could be counterproductive to the commitment to one another, God (cause I'm invoking the spirit), or the marriage. Temptation is not good, no matter its form. So, in constructive decision making, just as one would avoid a snake patch to minimize the likelihood of getting bit, he/she should also avoid the temptation to betray the commitment.

Contrary to what many internet cheaters and would be internet cheaters state, internet relationships are cheating-PERIOD. First, it is deceitful. Now if both agree that it is o.k. then that is fine. But, if you have hidden it-which means that you have made an effort to make sure your wife or husband cannot find it, if you cannot access it with your wife or husband present or milling around, if you have had to create an email address or gotten a cell phone specifically to keep that, or made sure that the charge does not say what site it is actually from, if it takes time from your work because you can't do it at home, consumes your social life, or takes away from the marriage, if it is deceptive (because your husband or wife cannot access the info and would feel violated by the content), and it involves intimacy-even when it is not physical-be it sex talk, nude picture or video sharing, flirtation, it is cheating and a violation of the commitment and marriage. It is a form of interaction, connection, and communication that takes away from the marriage because it generates a "relationship" not a friendship that is counterproductive to the marital connection, and serves as a temptation for infidelity. I don't want any other woman romantically occupying my husband's mind but me. Call it what you want, but I should, in my commitment to him, make sure I keep myself up, my sexual and intimate relationship spicy, and contribute to our mutual satisfaction. And the same should apply for and to me.

Friends and connections with people who you know (even if you don't admit it) like and or are interested in you-whether they can smile in your wife's or husbands face or not. NO!!!!NO!!!!NO!!!!!AND A HELL TO THE NAW!!!!!! I must say that I have seen some scandalous shit in my life, both personally and professionally. So, I know that people can and do come to the house, smile in the spouses face, and conspire against him/her. I also know that there is something alluring about "the possibility" of another, of knowing that someone other than the one you're with feels you-even if it is a rejected advance on the street. It is an ego boost that doesn't become an issue until there is conflict in the marriage. Why, because "friends" create options to resolving conflict in the marriage-clearly. Even your girls and your boys create that welcome distraction. But, you can't cross the line with them, although they may encourage you to do so with another. You can hate and produce that negativity, but you can't cross the line with them. That cell phone with the "friends" numbers(s) in it is often the first thing people go to when they are going through something. It is the distraction that gives people an excuse to turn away from- instead of into a marriage. Rationalize it, intellectualize it, make it seem right-those types of "friends" have no place in a marriage.

The way I look at it, true friends have your best interest in mind and at heart. And, people with values and morals, and don't get mad if this is you, do NOT pursue or even accept the advances of (OPP) other people's husbands and wives. So as a husband or wife, why would you even want to risk your marriage on someone that you meet on the internet, work, the club, the gym, or even the strip club that would go there? The greatness in you does not change the character of the one that makes you "feel special." So, other than sex and a physical and emotional high that will lead to a crazy crash, what could you possibly get from such a connection? Seriously.

These are just some of the core things that I believe lend to a healthy marriage. It is not gospel and is grounded in my "perfessional" opinion. It is designed to be a guide to promoting a solid foundation. I hope it helps.

Final Chapter
Mo Betta'

Cheese gets mo betta wit time

Roses get mo betta wit time

Wine gets mo betta wit time

Wounds get mo betta wit time

Heart ache gets mo betta wit time

Money wisely invested gets mo betta wit time

Intelligence gets mo betta wit time

Consciousness gets mo betta wit time

Connections get mo betta wit time

Love gets mo betta wit time

Making love gets mo betta wit time

Life gets mo betta wit time

I get mo betta wit time

We, get mo betta wit time!

This has been a most cathartic journey, even for me. In my quest to not only find answers that satisfy me but to develop my own sense of self so that I will be prepared for my soul mate, I have extended my views to you through this work. It's hard core and sometimes brutal. It will touch and challenge. But both are necessary because it is only through challenge that we grow and only through growth that we actualize.

As women (and men), we have to begin to re-shape and regain control over how we define our "selves" as such. We have to regain control over how we allow our presentations and images to be manipulated and distributed by the media and other social and political organisms. But, most importantly we have to find the strength to be true to self so that we can be true to others. Only then can we begin to command love and all that grows from it.

As humans, we are delicate creatures with great power- power that we fail to develop or utilize to guide or destiny. In such, many of us go through life in and out of a series of relationships that cause more and more heartbreak- relationships that make it more and more difficult for us to even embrace love and even conceptualize the possibility of beautiful relationships.

Life is not meant to be lived in mediocrity. It is not meant to be skated through. We all have purpose and meaning in this space. In our lives there is infinite possibility that we can only realize through our own actualization. When we develop our "selves," define who we want to be and what we want out of life, and then actively engage in it, we can reach greatness. While we allow others to define and guide our paths and destinies like puppets, we remain stagnant-as perhaps it is meant.

Gaining control over one's life is inherent with time. We don't remain children, dependent on parents forever. We are given through the development of our "selves" the capacity to shape our destinies. When we connect to our Higher Power, our path and destiny will be lit by a divine light that makes it clearer. That is why it is important not to be immersed in the "murky depths" of our own stagnation.

Just like wine gets better with time, just like wounds heal better with time, just like intelligence and consciousness get better with time, just like heartbreak gets better with time, so does life. We all have the capacity to get better with time. The question is who will? Well here is to the great possibility of developing love for self, gaining the love of another, and knowing beautiful relationships that truly end "happily ever after." So, here's to the end of playing games and being lost. Here's to the end of heartbreak and disappointment. Here's to the end of *"thinking like a man!" Here's to the end of Women Talk Too Damn Much! And here's to Love!*

183